Published by
Random House Australia Pty Ltd
20 Alfred Street, Milsons Point, NSW 2061
http://www.randomhouse.com.au

Sydney   New York   Toronto
London   Auckland   Johannesburg
and agencies throughout the world

First published in 1998
Copyright © Kirsten McKay 1998

National Library of Australia
Cataloguing-in-Publication Data

McKay, Kirsten
Café Café

ISBN 0 09 183728 6.
1. Cookery. I. Title
641.5

Design by Gayna Murphy, Greendot Design
Typeset by Asset Typesetters, Sydney
Printed in Hong Kong by South China Printing Company (1988) Ltd.

10 9 8 7 6 5 4 3 2 1

Café
Café

Café

A COOKBOOK FOR THE EASY LIFE

BY KIRSTEN McKAY

PHOTOGRAPHY BY JOHN HOLLINGSHEAD

RANDOM HOUSE
AUSTRALIA

My greatest teacher and dearest friend

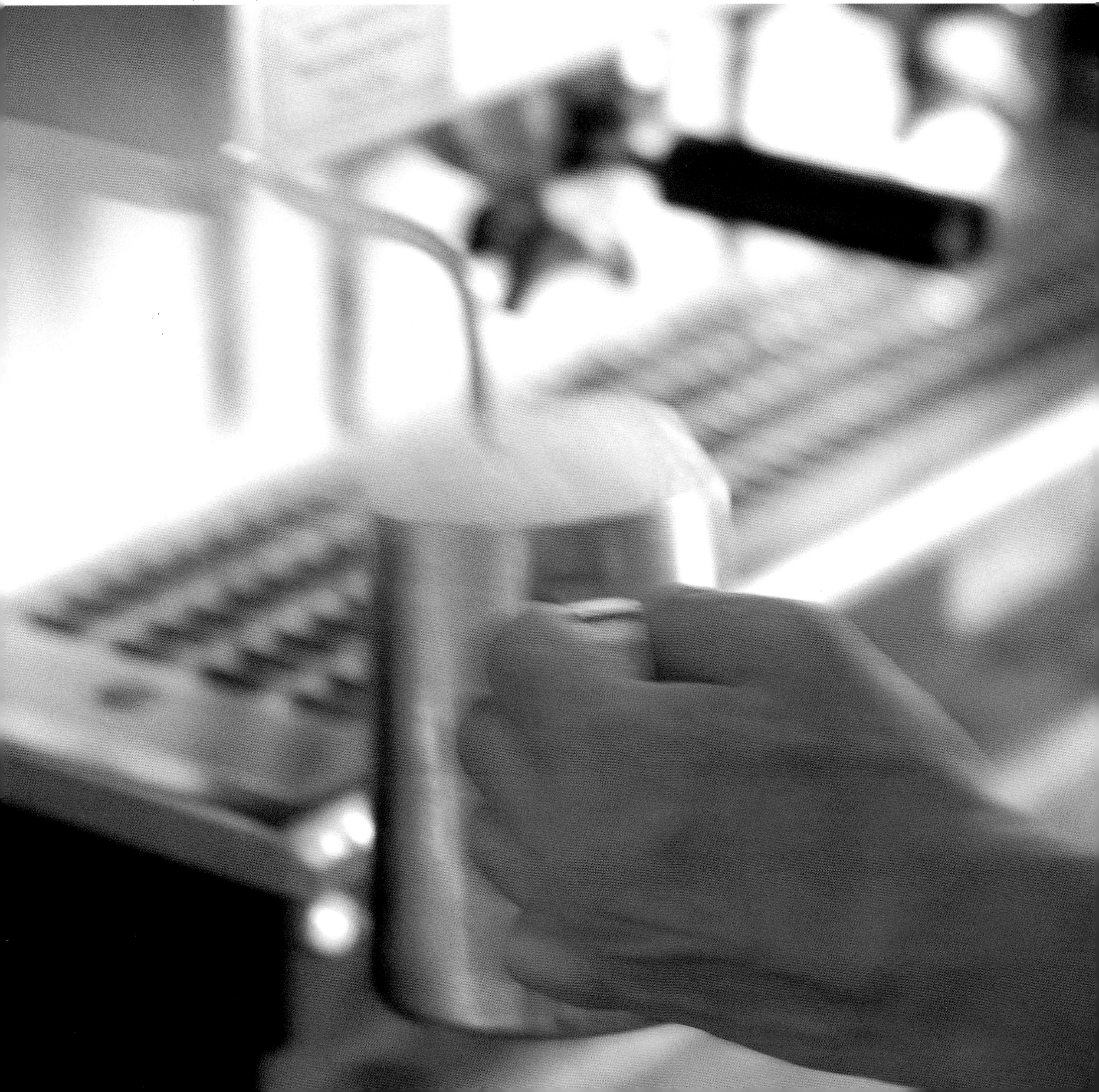

Contents

ACKNOWLEDGEMENTS

So many people to thank, not just for their incredible assistance in creating this book, but for a working life that has been greatly enriched and supported by some very talented and creative people.

Special thanks go to my two grandmothers Biddy Bayliss and Susan Joyce McKay, Patrick Breheny, Alain Chagney, David Thompson, Peter Bowyer, Peter Doyle, Steve and Franca Manfredi, Jo Collard, Mick Norris, June Moore, Carole Baker, Robyn Thurston, Pat Birley, Jenny Lopez, Nathan Fasan, and a very special thanks to Andrew Towns.

I'm deeply indebted to Anders Ousback who, quite apart from being the most inspired, humorous and generous of human beings, has changed the face of food and restaurant life in Sydney forever, and so much for the better.

Thomas Street Café, for me, was the culmination of many years of hard work and the team of staff that kept it alive and successful remain very special to me. There were many of you over the years; my particular gratitude to Zema, Linda, Nathan, Jamies 1 and 2, Mick, Görel and, of course, our loyal clientele. Thomas Street Café continues under the talented eye of Greg Higgs who offered his valuable cooperation with this book.

The enthusiasm and commitment of Deb Callaghan at Random House in getting Café Café off the ground can not be overstated, I am deeply indebted to her for her perseverance and loyalty. Special thanks also to Gayna Murphy for her inspired design, editor Linda Venturoni-Wilson for her painstaking work, Jody Lee for keeping the show on the road and Lisa Hanrahan.

Almost last, but far from least, my heartfelt thanks to John Hollingshead for his energetic devotion to capturing my food in pictures – it has been a pleasure working with you.

Finally, a big thank you to my family who know exactly what this all means to me.

And all my love to Felix.

FOREWORD

I am not at all impressed with Kirsten McKay's latest book. Having owned, operated and consulted for a good couple of dozen eating houses it would have been of immense help to have had, at hand, a book so brimming with simple, fresh, innovative, delicious and creative dishes.

But it wasn't.

Nobody knows the truffles I've seen.

ANDERS OUSBACK

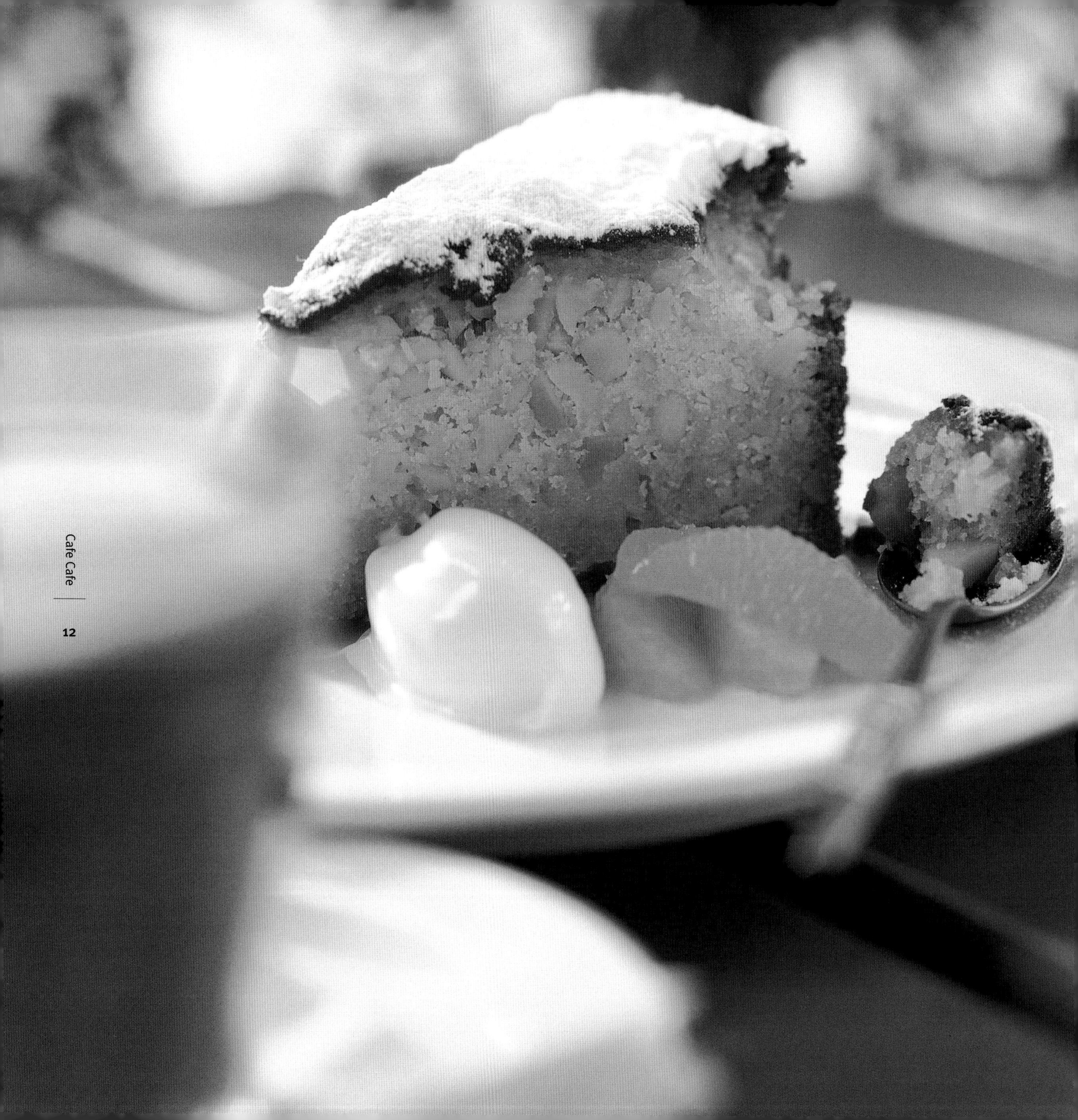

intro

Taking plastic cutlery from his pocket and positioning it carefully at his usual table, he realises that something is very wrong. A wave of anxiety comes over him. His favourite waitress is not at the café today. In the film As Good As It Gets, we soon see Jack Nicholson's character, Melvin Udal, turn up at the doorstep of the said waitress proclaiming his hunger.

Would this scene have worked set around the faceless facade of a fast food outlet? I don't think so. Would it seem as plausible if the waitress worked in a fine restaurant? At a pinch, maybe. But it wouldn't be the same.

There's a middle ground between the ever-burgeoning junk food industries and the heady heights of fine cuisine that caters for our need to find somewhere, in the everyday flow of things, that we can be comfortable and hungry. With food, when we seek out qualities like friendliness, familiarity and informality, we turn firstly to our own homes and then, to cafés.

Or, do we? Australians seem to be turning more and more to the cafés and modest restaurants before they consider their own homes, a development that is slowly eroding at our collective cooking skills. The flourishing home-delivery services may bode well for the maintenance of home-based family unity or they may just reflect the importance of television and the need to wind down after a long day. Whatever the case, they do little for our abilities in the kitchen.

This book, by no means alone, is part of a call to keep home cooking alive and creative. A call to take the lessons learned behind the closed doors of restaurant and café kitchens that have been busy responding to the ever more sophisticated tastes of the public, and bringing that food into our own homes – via our kitchens, not the front door!

Having suggested that culinary skills are in decline, I'll stand by my other claim, that the Australian sense of taste has become increasingly well-honed. Customers have steadily come to expect higher and higher standards for their lunchtime dollar and, in a country that now boasts some two hundred different spoken languages, we can hardly be surprised at the range of styles and flavours to be found. With our televisions bringing us sights and sounds from every corner of the globe, we want our cafés to do the same with taste.

Café menus appear to be moving closer and closer to that hazy line that divides cafés from restaurants. But the simple truth is that the line has always been hazy. When we cast a historical glance over our shoulders, we quickly discover that the defining qualities of a café have never been very clear. French for coffee, the word 'café' has come to embrace a host of meanings across different times and cultures.

Let's start at the beginning – where does the word café actually come from? One legend tells us that, somewhere around 850 AD, an Arab goat herd named Kaldi couldn't help but notice the somewhat frenetic behaviour of his flock whenever they consumed the berries of a particular bush. If we are to beli eve this, the humble beginnings of caffeine consumption seem to have taken place near the town of Kefa in Ethiopia. Kefa, café, coffee – fair enough – but how did café come to mean 'a small and informal establishment serving various refreshments'?

Greeted variously with protest and approval by religious orders and medical professions alike, coffee started appearing in Europe towards the end of the seventeenth century. It proved to be a taste that was easily acquired and by the turn of the century coffee houses could be found throughout Europe. Naturally enough, in France these became known as cafés. Among the sweeping reforms of the French Revolution in 1789 came the removal of aristocratic privileges, which frequently seemed to include their heads. Quite apart from anything else, these events saw an unprecedented number of private chefs seeking alternative means of employment. That over five hundred restaurants had opened in Paris alone, all within a mere fifteen years, indicates one particularly popular solution found by the culinary labour force. That many of these were called cafés tells us that the 'hazy line' was there from the very beginning.

The mid to late nineteenth century was to be the golden age of the café and the name could be found adorning anything from a simple workman's coffee house to such extravagent establishments of la belle époque' as Café Paris and the Grand Café de Foy. 'The bourgeosie want an imitation of their drawing room, the workers a replica of their parlour … with food just like homecooking' says Marie-France Boyer in her book, *The French Café*. It seems that everyone wanted a second living room that reflected something of their own homes whether for purposes of discussing the weather or re-defining art, politics and philosophy. Across the Atlantic, however, the name café could be found on something very different altogether.

One night in 1872, Walter Scott (as opposed to Sir Walter Scott who died forty years earlier) was to be found making his inaugural trip down Westminster Street of Providence, Rhode Island at the reins of a horsedrawn wagon loaded with sandwiches, pies and, you've guessed it, coffee. The Night Lunch Cart came into existence to supply the demand of hungry nightworkers ill-served by restaurants that closed at 8 p.m. It was a runaway success. Soon wagons were being built with seating for several inside and room for more to stand. They were called cafés. You'd hardly expect the decor of these cafés-on-wheels to match that of the more opulent Parisian variety, where grand mirrors, marble-top tables, painted glass and highly ornate, gilded embellishments were the norm, but they actually came surprisingly close. The 'luxury model' of the mass-produced White House Café, for example, had stained glass windows and panels carrying highly intricate paintings of landscapes and historical scenes. In the fullness of time the wheels were replaced by foundations of brick and mortar – and so was born the American diner.

Now we can see, from the briefest of strolls through history, that it would take nothing short of a small library dedicated to the food of the last three or four centuries to fully embrace all that ever graced a café menu. I'm pleased to say that I've given myself a simpler task, setting out to capture the food that I personally served at my own café, Thomas Street Café, in North Sydney somewhere towards the end of the twentieth century. Having said that, the echoes and contributions of many different cultures are to be found throughout these pages, from Croque Monsieur to Burgers, from Pad Thai Noodles to Antipasto, from Gnocchi to Gumbo Ya Ya.

Oddly enough, given the caffeine connection, this is not a cook book intended for the coffee table, rubbing shoulders with travel books full of photos that you're probably just as unlikely to visit on any regular basis. This is a book to use. I've kept the recipes as simple as possible, whilst retaining the integrity of the end result. So make this book yours. Make it work for you. Plunder the basics section for all it's worth and fill your fridge with goodies ready-to-go. Prepare entire meals in advance and shatter the illusion that your local café always cooks your favourite dish to order. Give yourself full permission to make it as easy for yourself as possible. For some, that means following each direction to the letter, for others it means taking all manner of shortcuts, such as using commercial pastes and sauces in place of individual herbs and spices. There is no right way. There'll be others who are compelled to make the most individual, and sometimes bizarre, detours from the recipes, occasionally breaking new ground. To those of you in this last category; please send me a postcard whenever you discover lost civilisations or new taste sensations on your travels. I'd love to hear from you.

If there's no right way to cook, how do we know when we're going in the right direction? Well, how do we know if we like a café? For me, it's when I can enjoy satisfying the simple desire to eat in physical and financial comfort. There's an enduring need for the comfort zone simplicity of the lived-in café, but much more than that, we must be sure of finding these same qualities in our own homes.

So, how will you know if this book works for you? It won't be a chore – you'll be enjoying yourself.

breakfast

* Lemon and Walnut Bread
* Best Banana and Almond Bread
* Breakfast Rösti
* Sultana, Date and Oat Cakes with Fruit Salad and Yoghurt
* Baked Ricotta with Cinnamon and Honey with Warm Compote of Fruit
* French Toast with Grilled Bacon and Bananas
* Eggs Benedict with Ham or Smoked Salmon
* Croque Monsieur
* Potato Latkes with Warm Apple Sauce
* Scrambled Eggs with Corn Muffins
* Baked Eggs with Glazed Tomatoes and Toast
* Smoked Haddock Kedgeree
* Zema's Banana Smoothie
* Fresh Fruit Frappé
* Orange and Lime Zinger

LEMON AND WALNUT
BREAD

MAKES 2 LOAVES

4	Eggs – separated
	Pinch of salt
250g	Unsalted butter
1$^1/_2$ cups (375g)	Sugar
$^1/_2$ cup	Lemon juice
2$^1/_2$ cups (310g)	Plain flour
3 tsp	Baking powder
1 cup	Milk
1 cup (125g)	Walnuts – chopped

LEMON GLAZE:

1/2 cup (125g)	Sugar
	Juice of 3 lemons.

Preheat the oven to moderately slow 160°C. Butter and flour two loaf tins (25 x 10cm) .

Whisk the egg whites with a pinch of salt to form soft peaks and set to one side.

Beat the butter and sugar together until creamy. Add the egg yolks and beat until blended thoroughly. Stir in the lemon juice.

Combine the flour and baking powder and fold into the creamed mixture alternately with the milk.

Fold in the walnuts, then fold in the beaten egg whites. Pour the mixture into the prepared tins.

Bake for 25 minutes or until a skewer comes out clean. Remove from the oven and turn onto a cooling rack.

To make the lemon glaze, stir the lemon juice and sugar in a small saucepan over medium heat until the sugar dissolves and a light syrup forms. The syrup should be poured over the bread whilst hot.

Extremely more-ish. I recommend making two loaves and freezing one ... just in case.

Best Banana
and Almond Bread

MAKES 1 LARGE LOAF

2	Bananas – mashed
$^1/_4$ cups (30g)	Almonds – chopped
$1^1/_2$ cups (375mL)	Sour cream
$1^3/_4$ cups (220g)	Plain flour
1 tsp	Baking powder
125g	Unsalted butter – melted
1 cup (250g)	Sugar
2	Eggs
$^1/_2$ cup (60g)	Sultanas
2 tsp	Ground cinnamon
1 tsp	Bicarbonate of soda (baking soda)
$^1/_4$ (55g)	Firmly packed brown sugar

Preheat the oven to 180ºC. Butter and flour a loaf tin (25 x 10cm).

In a large bowl, mix together the sour cream and bicarbonate of soda. Set to one side for 5 minutes then stir in the melted butter, sugar and eggs.

In another bowl, combine the flour, baking powder and cinnamon. Gradually whisk in the sour cream mixture and finally fold in the bananas and sultanas. Pour the mixture into the prepared tin.

Mix together the brown sugar and almonds and sprinkle over the top of the batter. Bake for 1 to $1^1/_4$ hours or until a skewer comes out clean. Cool in the tin for 20 minutes before turning out onto a cooling rack.

This bread is delicious toasted under the grill and served with lashings of butter.

BREAKFAST RÖSTI

SERVES 4

2	Parsnips (large)
500g	Potatoes
	(pontiacs or desiree) – peeled
300g	Celeriac – peeled
2 tbls	Olive oil
4	Eggs (free-range)
1 cup (125g)	Cheddar – grated
	Fresh thyme
	Parsley – chopped
	Salt and pepper

Preheat the oven to 200°C.

Cook the potatoes, parsnips and the celeriac together in a saucepan of boiling, lightly salted water until just soft. Drain and cool until easy to handle, then grate the vegetables into a bowl. Add the cheese, oil and herbs to taste, season with salt and black pepper and mix together thoroughly.

Lightly oil an ovenproof frying pan. Spoon in the potato mixture, making four slight indentations in the middle with the back of a spoon. Bake for 15–20 minutes until the potatoes are turning golden and crispy.

Remove the rösti from the oven and break the eggs into the hollows. Return to the oven for a further 10 minutes to set eggs.

Serve immediately with toasted whole wheat bread.

A fine dice of bacon can be added to the mixture if desired.

I fell in love with this dish on my honeymoon in Nepal. Though it is hardly a traditional Nepalese dish, it never fails to conjure up views of the Himalayas in my mind.

SULTANA, DATE AND OAT CAKES
WITH FRUIT SALAD AND YOGHURT
SERVES 6

$^3/_4$ cup (125g)	Almonds – chopped
$^1/_3$ cup (50g)	Sesame seeds
1 cup (125g)	Sultanas
$^1/_2$ cup (100g)	Dried apricots – chopped
$^2/_3$ cup (125g)	Dried dates – chopped
$1^1/_2$ cup (150g)	Rolled oats
1 cup (150g)	Wholemeal flour
$^1/_3$ cup (75g)	Raw sugar
$^2/_3$ cup (175mL)	Apple or pear juice
1 tbls	Honey
$^1/_3$ cup (75mL)	Vegetable oil

FOR SERVING

	Fresh fruit of your choice, such as mangoes, strawberries, melon, peaches
1 tub (200g)	Greek-style plain yoghurt

Preheat the oven to 180°C. Grease and line a baking tin (25 x 30cm) with baking paper.

In a large bowl combine all the ingredients except the fresh fruit and yoghurt. Press this mixture gently into the prepared tin and bake for 40–45 minutes, until firm and golden.

While still hot, cut the slice into 12 squares but leave in the tin until completely cool before turning out.

Serve with fresh fruit salad and drizzled with yoghurt.

These oatcakes are great for a light, simple breakfast and will keep for 3–4 days in a well sealed jar. You can also use them as a lunchtime snack for the kids.

BAKED RICOTTA
WITH CINNAMON AND HONEY
WITH WARM COMPOTE OF FRUIT

SERVES 6

FOR THE RICOTTA:

750g	Fresh ricotta
2	Eggs
2 tbls	Honey
1 tsp	Cinnamon

COMPOTE OF FRUIT:

2 cups (375g)	Mixed dried fruit
2 tbls	Brown sugar
2 tbls	Honey
1	Cinnamon quill
2	Bay leaves
3	Cloves
$^1/_2$	Vanilla pod – split
	Juice of 1 orange
	Zest of $^1/_2$ lemon

To cook ricotta:
Preheat the oven to 150ºC.

In a large bowl whisk together the ricotta, eggs, honey, and cinnamon. Pour this mixture into a non-stick loaf tin (25 x 10cm) and cover with aluminium foil. Now place this tin in a large baking tin filled with warm water to come halfway up the side of the loaf tin. Bake for 45–60 minutes, or until firm.

It is easier to turn out the ricotta when it is cool.

To cook the compote:
Place all the ingredients in a large pot. Cover with water and bring to the boil. Simmer gently for 10 minutes, then take away from the heat and allow to cool in the syrup.

Serve the compote warm with the sliced ricotta.

This can be made in advance and kept in the refrigerator for 2 weeks.

The warm, spicy flavours combined with the richness of baked ricotta make for a wonderful Sunday breakfast in winter.

breakfast

FRENCH TOAST
WITH GRILLED BACON AND BANANAS
SERVES 4

8 slices	White bread
	(preferably, not pre-sliced bread)
4	Eggs
$^1/_3$ cup	(80mL) Cream
4 rashers	Bacon
4	Bananas
	Maple syrup
	Butter for cooking
	Icing sugar, for dusting

Grill the bacon to suit your personal taste.

Peel and split the bananas lengthways, dust with icing sugar and gently rub in a little bit of butter to help them caramelise. Place the bananas onto a flat baking tray that will fit under your grill and cook till they are golden and soft but still holding their shape. (If you don't have a grill, gently fry them in a little butter in a non-stick frying pan).

In a bowl, whisk together the eggs and the cream. In a large non-stick frying pan, gently melt some butter and add the bread that has been generously passed through the egg mix. Cook on both sides till golden and serve immediately with the crispy bacon, grilled bananas and maple syrup.

The Secret
Use bread that is a little on the stale side, it absorbs the egg mix better.

Not a breakfast for the faint hearted!

EGGS BENEDICT
WITH HAM OR SMOKED SALMON

SERVES 4

4	English muffins
4	Slices of ham off the bone or smoked salmon
8	Free-range eggs for poaching

HOLLANDAISE SAUCE:

250g	Unsalted butter
4 tbls	Good quality white wine vinegar
2 tbls	White wine
1	Bay leaf
2	Black peppercorns
4	Egg yolks
2 tbls	Sparkling mineral water (optional)
	Juice of $^1/_2$ lemon

To pepare the hollandaise, melt the butter gently (do not boil) and allow it to cool slightly.

In a small saucepan, place the vinegar, white wine, bay leaf, and peppercorns. Reduce this liquid to approximately 2 tablespoons.

In a stainless steel bowl that fits snugly over a small saucepan of boiling water, add the egg yolks and the reduced liquid. Whisk continually over a gentle heat, until the yolks are thick and foaming. Turn off the boiling water at this stage, but leave the bowl over the saucepan. Now, gently begin to whisk in the melted butter. It is important not to do this too quickly or the hollandaise will split.

When all the butter has been incorporated, you can add the mineral water if you wish; this helps make a light, fluffy hollandaise. Add the lemon juice to taste and season well with salt and pepper. Keep warm (not hot) till needed.

Poach the eggs only enough so that they are held together, but with a yolk that is still soft and runny. If using ham, trim the fat and take the chill off it slightly. Do not cook as this will alter the flavour completely. Toast the muffins and butter them.

To assemble, place either the ham or the smoked salmon on the buttered muffins. Place the eggs on top and finish with the warm hollandaise sauce. Serve immediately.

The Secret
The quality of eggs benedict depend on the ingredients—good fresh eggs and good quality ham or smoked salmon are essential—but most important of all is the hollandaise sauce.

Leaving one beautifully satisfied (and perhaps feeling slightly wicked!), this has got to be one of the most universally loved breakfasts.

CROQUE MONSIEUR
SERVES 4

8 slices	White bread
8 slices	Ham off the bone
8 slices	Gruyére
2	Free-range eggs
3 tbls	Cream
	Butter for frying

Spread the bread with Dijon mustard to taste. Then layer with the ham and cheese to create four full and generous sandwiches.

In a bowl, whisk together the eggs and the cream.

In a large, non-stick frying pan, melt enough butter to gently fry the sandwiches.

Passing each sandwich through the egg mix, cook gently on each side until golden brown and the cheese has melted. If the cheese needs more time, place the croque monsieur in the oven to warm through. Serve hot.

For Croque Madame:
Do exactly as for croque monsieur and serve with a fried egg on top.

This is a variation of the Parisian café classic. Delicious for breakfast, or as a snack.

POTATO LATKES
WITH WARM APPLE SAUCE
SERVES 6

7	Potatoes (large, red skinned)
2	Eggs (large) – beaten
2	Onions (small)
1	Granny Smith apple
1 cup (150g)	Plain flour
	Pinch of ground cinnamon
1 tsp	Salt
	Pinch of black pepper
	Vegetable oil for shallow frying
APPLE SAUCE:	
10	Granny Smith apples – peeled and cut into small chunks
	Juice of 2 oranges
$^1/_2$ cup (125g)	Raw sugar
$^1/_2$ tsp	Ground cinnamon
$^1/_2$ tsp	Ground cloves
	Plain yoghurt for serving

Grate the potatoes, onions and apple, then place in a tea towel and squeeze out the excess liquid.

Place the mixture in a bowl and mix in the eggs, salt, cinnamon, pepper and flour.

Heat the oil in a large frying pan and drop in spoonfuls of the batter and cook until golden brown on both sides. Allow to drain on absorbent paper.

Keep warm in a 120°C oven while cooking the remaining mixture.

To make the apple sauce, place all the ingredients in a heavy-based saucepan.

Cook uncovered over a medium to low heat till the apples have totally softened and are mushy. Serve the latkes with the warm apple sauce and yoghurt.

The contrast of crisp latkes with soft, sweet apple sauce creates the magic of this wonderful German breakfast.

SCRAMBLED EGGS
WITH CORN MUFFINS
SERVES 4

8	Eggs
$^1/_4$ cup (60mL)	Cream
2 tbls	Butter
1 bunch	Chives – chopped
	Salt and pepper
	FOR THE MUFFINS:
5	Bacon rashers
1	Small onion – finely chopped
1 cup (150g)	Plain flour
1 cup (150g)	Polenta
3 tbls	Sugar
1 tbls	Baking powder
	Salt
2	Free-range eggs
1 cup (250mL)	Milk
1 tin (420g)	Corn kernels – drained
	A handful chopped parsley

Preheat the oven to 190ºC. Grease a muffin tray.

Slice the bacon and fry it until crisp then drain on absorbent paper and cool.

Sauté the onions In the bacon fat and set to one side.

In a mixing bowl, mix the flour, polenta, sugar, baking powder, and salt.

In another small bowl whisk together the eggs and milk.

Add the egg mixture to the flour and mix in thoroughly. Then fold through the corn kernels, bacon, onion, and parsley.

Spoon the mixture into the prepared muffin tray and bake for 15 minutes or until a skewer comes out clean.

To prepare the scrambled eggs, in a bowl, mix the eggs and cream together gently with a fork. In a large non-stick frying pan, place the butter and pour in the egg mix. Cook over a gentle heat and, with a wooden spoon, gently bring the cooked egg into the centre and continue doing so till the egg is scrambled and creamy to suit your personal taste. Season well with salt and pepper, garnish with the chives and serve with the warm corn muffins.

A good Southern American start to the day. The muffins can be made in advance and frozen.

Baked Eggs
with Glazed Tomatoes and Toast
Serves 4

For the eggs:

4	Free-range eggs
4 tbls	Spicy Tomato Chutney (see Basics page 149)
4 tbls	Chopped fresh herbs, such as basil, parsley, chives
	Cream
	Salt and pepper
	Wood-fired bread, sliced and toasted
4	Ramekins – buttered

Glazed Tomatoes:

6	Roma tomatoes
3 tbls	Olive oil
$1^1/_2$ tbls	Balsamic vinegar
	Brown sugar
	Thyme (fresh)
	Salt and pepper

Preheat the oven to 160ºC.

Cut the tomatoes in half lengthways. Lay them on a flat baking tray and drizzle with the olive oil and balsamic vinegar. Sprinkle with the brown sugar, thyme, and salt and pepper to taste. Bake for 1 hour, or until they soften and glaze.

To prepare the eggs, increase the oven temperature to 180ºC. Divide the tomato chutney and the mixed herbs between four buttered ramekins. Break an egg on top of this mixture in each ramekin and then cover with cream. Season well and bake for 10–12 minutes. The eggs need to be firm but not hard. Serve with the glazed tomatoes and wood-fired bread toast.

Variations

Substitute the tomato chutney with any of the following:

* Sautéed mushrooms

* Bacon and onion

* Smoked salmon and dill

* Ham and cheese

Smoked Haddock Kedgeree

Serves 6

1²/₃ cups (300g)	Basmati rice – boiled
500g	Smoked haddock fillets
250g	Salmon fillets – cut into cubes
4	Eggs – hard-boiled and quartered
1	Onion – finely chopped
2 sticks	Celery – finely chopped
2 cloves	Garlic – minced
1 bunch	Coriander
45g	Butter
2 cups (500mL)	Milk
1 cup (250mL)	Cream
1 tsp	Ginger – minced
1 stick	Cinnamon quill
2	Cardamom pods
3	Cloves
1 tsp	Fennel seeds
1 tsp	Ground cumin
1 tsp	Turmeric
	Salt and pepper

} or a tablespoon of your favourite curry powder or or paste

In a large frying pan, bring the milk to the boil, reduce the heat and add the smoked haddock fillets. Poach gently for 3 minutes. Remove the fish from the milk and allow to cool down before breaking the flesh away from the bones. Set to one side.

In another large frying pan, melt the butter and sauté the onion with the celery, garlic, ginger and spices for a couple of minutes.

Add the cream and simmer gently for a few more minutes. Now add the rice and salmon and cook, stirring, for a few further minutes. Once the rice is thoroughly mixed with the onions, add the flaked fish, fresh coriander and boiled eggs. Adjust seasoning to taste and serve hot.

I first came across kedgeree whilst catering for balls and weddings in London where, usually at around 2 a.m. in the morning, tradition has it that everyone is served with kedgeree for 'breakfast,'— to re-energize, and soak up the booze, no doubt.

The classic kedgeree of the British Raj was developed as a way of using up leftover curry and rice.

ZEMA'S BANANA SMOOTHIE

SERVES 2

2	Ripe bananas
1 cup (250mL)	Milk
1 cup (250g)	Yoghurt
2 tbls	Honey
	Pinch of ground cinnamon
	Ice

Place all the ingredients into a blender and process till smooth and fluffy.

FRESH FRUIT FRAPPÉ

SERVES 2

1 cup	Prepared fresh fruit, such as berries, melons, pineapple, pears
	Ice
1 cup (250mL)	Orange juice

Place all the ingredients into a blender and process till smooth.

ORANGE AND LIME ZINGER

SERVES 2

4	Oranges – peeled
	Juice of 2 limes
1	Punnet strawberries – hulled
	Ice

Put all the ingredients into a blender and process till smooth.

antip

and crostini toppings

* Antipasto
* Tzatziki
* Hummus
* Muhamarra
* Babaghanoush
* Zucchini, Mustard and Avocado Dip

asto

Not a grand, swanky '3 star' in France, or some chic and trendy outfit in London, this little restaurant was of the simple 'wooden table and Paris goblet' tradition—but it was mind-blowing for me. A ceiling obscured by prosciuttos, salamis, sausages and cheeses. A waiter's table overwhelmed by crusty wood-fired breads and crostinis. Down the centre of the room, a long, wooden table spilling over with colour, platter upon platter of the most beautiful antipasto I had ever seen or dreamt.

Communal antipasto tables will no doubt linger in the memories of most travellers to Italy, but what was different about this little restaurant tucked away in the back streets of Rome was that antipasto was all they served! As a committed nibbler, this was my idea of heaven—short flavoursome bursts of self-selected, beautifully prepared dishes. Yum.

I always thought the idea would translate to Sydney extremely well. I remain convinced, but one thing and another lead me to realising Thomas Street Café instead. There, naturally enough, antipasto became part of the established tradition.

Antipasto is a book in itself, so I shall limit myself here by simply referring to some of my favourite items, leaving it to your capable tastes and fancy to explore both your imagination and your local delicatessen.

Quality of produce is a clear and obvious requirement of good antipasto—fresh bread, good meats, seasonal vegetables, well flavoured olive oil. It is, however, worth remembering that antipasto can also be an excellent way of using up leftovers—leftover frittata, risottos (made into cakes and fried), roasted vegetables, cold meats, the list is endless.

Typical of Australian cuisine in general, the 'Australian antipasto' no longer recognises any cultural boundaries, borrowing flavours from such sources as Greek Mezzo and Spanish Tapas. More and more the tastes of Asia are finding their place alongside the more traditional European flavours. A distinguishing cafe trend of Australia has been the mixed crostini plate offering a selection of dips, spreads and pastes with freshly grilled bruschetta, dried crostinis or warm Turkish pide bread. While most of these are now mass produced, there's nothing better than a homemade hummus where you can finely tune the ingredients to your own taste. I've included recipes for several dips, some familiar, some not so familiar, at the end of this section.

So, with all of that in mind, here is my suggestion list for antipasto.

* Marinated artichokes with raspberry vinegar and sun-dried tomatoes (see recipe, page 66)

* Red and yellow capsicums roasted with roma tomatoes, olive oil and rosemary

* Seasonal fresh figs or rockmelon with prosciutto

* Grilled mushrooms with lemon zest, thyme and parsley (see Basics, Gremolata page 151)

* Finger eggplants roasted with garlic

* Roasted tomatoes with pesto (see Basics, page 147)

* Frittata with Potato and Asparagus, (see recipe page 60)

* Baked ricotta (see recipe, page 23) or Baked Ricotta and Pumpkin Salad

* Sardines marinated in lemon and olive oil

* Potato pancakes with smoked salmon, créme fraîche and salmon roe

* Banana Chillies roasted with Ricotta and Sun-dried Tomatoes (see recipe, page 86)

* Carpaccio of beef or kangaroo with rocket, parmesan and olive oil

* BBQ baby octopus with a touch of chilli and lime

* Tiny Mushroom and Pea Risotto Cakes (see recipe, page 98)

* Thai fish cakes with sweet cucumber relish

* Parmesan and gruyére crisps (see Basics, page 145)

* Broad bean, prosciutto and pecorino salad, with olive oil and parsley

* BBQ prawns wrapped in leeks

* Stuffed hard-boiled eggs, yolk mashed and mixed with Salsa Verde (see Basics, page 152)

* Squid filled with peperonata and braised in white wine and olive oil

* Seared tuna with capers, olives and lemon zest

* Rice paper rolls filled with prawns and water chestnuts

* BBQ duck with sweet plum sauce on pineapple pieces

* Deep-fried pork, coriander and ginger rice balls

* Scallops on the shell baked with ginger, spring onion and coriander

* Anchovies sandwiched with sage leaves, dipped in beer batter and deep-fried

* Baby bocconcini, marinated with pine nuts, oregano and lemon juice

* Salami fingers filled with grated beetroot, capers and horseradish

* Zucchini Pickle (see Basics, page 149)

* Caramelised Onions (see Basics, page 148)

* Finely shredded fresh carrot with hazelnuts and balsamic vinegar

* BBQ prawns in their shells with dill butter

* Yabbie tails with Spanish (red) onion and avocado

* Baby leeks braised with black olives, anchovies and thyme

* Grilled sardine fillets with Salsa Verde (see Basics, page 152)

* Roasted chat potatoes, scoop out the flesh, mix with Tapenade (see Basics, page 152) and refill

* Sautéed chicken livers on mini toasts with onion marmalade

* Roulade of eggplant, capsicum and goat's cheese (see recipe, page 85)

* Jerusalem artichokes cut in half, roasted and served with a grilled scallop and a dollop of mascarpone

* Puff pastry rounds baked with fetta, prawns and rosemary

Opposite page: Antipasto plate prepared by Greg Higgs, Thomas Street Café

TZATZIKI
YOGHURT AND CUCUMBER DIP

1 tub (200g)	Thick Greek-style yoghurt
1	Telegraph cucumber – peeled and grated
1-2 cloves	Garlic – minced
20	Fresh mint leaves – chopped finely
1 tbls	Olive oil
	Juice of 1 lemon
$^1/_4$ tsp	Ground cumin
$^1/_4$ tsp	Ground coriander
	Salt and pepper

Squeeze the grated cucumber in a tea towel to remove excess liquid.

Mix in a bowl with all the other ingredients adding salt to taste.

Cover and refrigerate till needed. Best eaten on the day it is made.

Hummus

1 cup (220g)	Chickpeas – soaked for 2 hours
2 cloves	Garlic
3 tbls	Tahini
	Juice of 1-2 lemons
2 tsp	Ground cumin
3 tbls	Olive oil
	Pinch of cayenne pepper
	Salt and pepper
	Parsley for garnish (optional)

Rinse the soaked chickpeas and cover in fresh, cold water. Bring to the boil and cook until very soft. Don't add any salt as this will keep the chickpeas hard.

Allow chickpeas to cool in the cooking water.

Process the chickpeas in a blender with a little of the cooking water, the garlic, cumin and salt and pepper. Add the tahini, lemon juice and more cooking water if needed.

Spoon the hummus onto a plate and finish with olive oil, cayenne pepper and freshly chopped parsley.

Taste is a personal thing — some people prefer less lemon and more tahini, others might shy away from the raw garlic, and so on. Play around with it until you find your own, individual blend.

CROSTINI TOPPINGS

MUHAMARRA

3 slices	White bread – toasted
1 1/2 cup (150g)	Walnuts – roasted lightly
2	Red capsicums – roasted, de-seeded and skinned (see Basics, page 147)
2	Carrots – peeled, cooked and puréed
2 cloves	Garlic – chopped finely
1	Green chilli (small) – chopped finely (optional)
1/3 cup (50g)	Pine nuts – roasted lightly
10	Fresh mint leaves
	A handful fresh coriander leaves
3 tbls	Olive oil
	Lemon juice

In a food processor, process the walnuts and toasted bread to the consistency of breadcrumbs.

Add the roasted capsicum, carrot purée, garlic and chilli and process to a thick purée.

With the machine still running, slowly add the olive oil and lemon juice.

Finally, add the pine nuts, mint and coriander. (The pine nuts want to stay pretty much intact, its just a case of mixing them through).

Cover and refrigerate till needed.

Rich and delicious, this Turkish dip is a little bit different from your usual dips.

BABAGHANOUSH

2-3	Eggplants (large)
2/3 cup (160g)	Tahini
2 cloves	Garlic – chopped finely
1 tbls	Ketjap manis (Indonesian sweet soy)
1 tbls	Spicy Tomato Chutney (see Basics, page 149)
1 tbls	Mayonnaise (good quality, preferably homemade, see Basics page 150)
	Juice of 1 lemon
	Salt and pepper

Preheat the oven to 180°C.

Roast the eggplants whole, until soft.

Remove from the oven and lay them on a naked gas flame for a few minutes, turning them as they become black and charred. This process is optional. However, it is entirely worth the extra effort, creating the true smoky flavour of this Middle Eastern dish.

Remove the flesh from the skin and put it in a food processor with the tahini, garlic and ketjap manis, tomato chutney and mayonnaise. Process roughly, (not a smooth paste), and finish with salt, pepper and lemon juice to taste.

The Secret
My version of babaghanoush has some clear differences from the traditional eggplant purée. The addition of Spicy Tomato Chutney has long been my 'secret ingredient'; one that many have asked me for. Try it.

ZUCCHINI, MUSTARD
AND AVOCADO DIP

1 tbls	Capers – chopped
2 cups	Zucchini – chopped
2 cloves	Garlic – chopped finely
1	Avocado – mashed
1	Green capsicum (small) – diced finely
1 tbls	Mayonnaise (good quality, preferably homemade, see Basics, page 150)
1 cm piece	Ginger – grated
2 tsp	Dijon mustard
1 tsp	Cider vinegar
1 tsp	Green shallot – chopped finely
10	Basil leaves – chopped finely
	Salt and pepper

Steam the zucchini lightly and purée it roughly. Strain to remove the excess liquid.

Mix through with all the other ingredients.

Season with salt and pepper and refrigerate till needed.

Mustard, capers and cider vinegar combine forces to bring out the subtle flavours of avocado and zucchini.

PUMPKIN AND COCONUT SOUP
WITH PRAWNS
SERVES 4–6

6 cups (1¹/₂ litres)	Chicken stock
12	Green prawns – shelled with tails left on
1¹/₂ kg	Pumpkin – cubed
2 sticks	Celery – finely sliced
1	Leek – sliced and washed thoroughly
2 cloves	Garlic – mashed
2cm piece	Ginger – grated
1 stalk	Lemon grass – bruised (white part only)
2	Kaffir lime leaves
2 cups	Coconut milk
3 tbls	Oil
¹/₂ bunch	Coriander leaves – chopped
	Salt and pepper
	Toasted peanuts
	Toasted shaved coconut (see Basics, page 148)

In a stockpot, heat 2 tablespoons oil and sauté the pumpkin, garlic, ginger, lemon grass, celery and leek for a few minutes.

Add the chicken stock and bring to the boil, adding the kaffir lime leaves and coconut milk. Simmer gently till the pumpkin is soft. Season with salt and pepper to taste.

In a frying pan, heat 1 tablespoon of oil and sauté the prawns till they turn pink.

Ladle the soup into bowls and garnish with the prawns, peanuts, coconut and chopped coriander.

The sweetness of the coconut milk and prawns team together and give an exotic twist to pumpkin soup.

soups

and bowls

* Pumpkin and Coconut Soup
* Spicy Lentil Soup with Cashews
* Thai Boat Soup
* Oxtail Soup
* Zucchini, Green Pea and Proscuitto Soup
* Chicken Laksa

SPICY LENTIL SOUP
WITH CASHEWS
SERVES 4–6

4 cups (1 Litre)	Chicken stock
1 cup (185g)	Small brown lentils – soaked
2	Potatoes – peeled and cut into smallish dice
2	Brown onions – chopped finely
2	Carrots – chopped into small dice
2 sticks	Celery – chopped finely
1	Granny Smith apple – peeled and cubed
350g tin	Italian roma tomatoes – chopped roughly
	Curry paste – to suit your taste
3 cloves	Garlic – chopped finely
2 cm piece	Ginger – chopped finely
2	Curry leaves
	Good pinch of cayenne pepper
2 tbls	Butter or vegetable oil
	Salt

GARNISH:

Roasted cashews

Fresh coriander

Plain yoghurt

Heat the butter or oil, in a large stockpot, add the curry paste and cook for a minute before adding the onions, garlic and ginger. Sweat these off for 2 minutes over low heat.

Add the lentils, potatoes, carrots, celery, apple and tomatoes. Mix well and add the stock and curry leaves.

Bring to the boil and then reduce the heat to cook gently for 40 minutes, or until the lentils are soft and tender.

Season well with salt and cayenne pepper.

Serve hot, garnished with roasted cashews, chopped coriander and a dollop of yoghurt.

Variation
Make this a more substantial meal with the addition of spiced meatballs that have been roasted or BBQ'd. The lamb kofta (see recipe page 131) would be fine, just use beef instead of lamb.

A hearty soup for a winter's lunch. Serve with garlic naan bread.

THAI BOAT SOUP

SERVES 4–6

1 kg	Fillet steak – frozen and then sliced very finely
6 cups (1^1/$_2$ Litres)	Beef stock
2^1/$_4$ cups (250g)	Bean sprouts
1 bunch	Baby bok choy
6	Green shallots – sliced finely
6	Eshalots – peeled
2 cups (500mL)	Water
2	Cinnamon quills
4 cm piece	Fresh ginger – sliced
2 cloves	Garlic
5 slices	Fresh galangal
3	Kaffir lime leaves
2-3	Birdseye chillies – chopped
2 stalks	Lemon grass – (white part only) sliced
2	Coriander roots – chopped (save leaves for garnish)
2	Star anise
2 tbls	Sweet chilli sauce
2 tbls	Fish sauce
2 tbls	Oyster sauce
^{1}/$_4$ bunch	Thai mint leaves – for garnish
1 tbls	Tamarind, prepared in 5 tbls (100mL) water – (see Glossary page 155)

In a large saucepan, place the stock, water, cinnamon, star anise, ginger, garlic, galangal, lime leaves, chillies, lemon grass and coriander roots. Bring to the boil and simmer gently for 25 minutes.

Strain the broth and discard all the spices, return the broth to the saucepan, adding the tamarind water, sweet chilli sauce, fish sauce, oyster sauce, and eshalot.

To serve:
While the broth is boiling, add the shaved beef, bean sprouts and bok choy. Cook for 1 minute only and then serve, garnished with coriander leaves, mint and spring onions.

Extra chilli should be served on the side for those partial to heat.

Oxtail Soup

SERVES 6

3–4 (3$\frac{1}{2}$kg approx.)	Oxtails – cut into pieces and trimmed of excess fat
	POACHING INGREDIENTS:
14 cups (3$\frac{1}{2}$ Litres)	Beef stock
2	Onions – chopped
2	Carrots (large) – chopped
2 sticks	Celery – chopped
2	Tomatoes – cut into quarters
4 cloves	Garlic – peeled and left whole
2 sprigs	Thyme
1	Bay leaf
1 piece	Orange zest
1 piece	Lemon zest
1 cup (250mL)	Red wine
	GARNISHING VEGETABLES:
1 bunch	Baby carrots – trimmed, peeled and boiled
4	Potatoes – boiled
6	Small brown pickling onions – halved and roasted
$\frac{2}{3}$ cup (115g)	Fresh broad beans – blanched and peeled of outer skin
	A handful of fresh mixed herbs – chopped finely

Preheat the oven to 180°C.

Brown the oxtails in a large roasting tin for 1 hour in the oven and transfer to a large stockpot.

Place the baking tin on a low heat and add the wine. With a wooden spoon, scrape the bottom of the pan to dislodge all the little sticky, meaty bits.

Pour the wine over the oxtails and add the onions, carrots, celery, tomatoes, garlic, herbs, zest and stock, it should generously cover the oxtails, so if it is a little short, top it off with some water.

Place on a high heat and bring to the boil, reducing heat to a low and gentle simmer. Cook for 1$\frac{1}{2}$–2 hours, skimming the skin and fat from the surface continually.

Strain the liquid off the meat and press all the ingredients through a fine sieve to get all the available juices. Discard the pulp and place the liquid into the refrigerator for a couple of hours to allow all the fat to surface. Protect the meat from drying out with a damp tea towel or absorbent paper. Once the fat has risen, remove it carefully with a spoon, and pour the sauce back over the meat.

Serve the oxtails garnished with the roasted onions, boiled potatoes and carrots, and the broad beans. Sprinkle with some finely chopped herbs.

Delicious eaten with some grilled polenta or crispy Italian wood-fired bread.

Pure joy and comfort food for the winter months, this is a substantial meal in itself. The butcher had a hard time keeping our cafe supplied as it used to walk off the menu.

ZUCCHINI, GREEN PEA
AND PROSCIUTTO SOUP

SERVES 4

1	Large leek – trimmed and sliced finely
2 tbls	Olive oil
500g	Zucchini
2 cloves	Garlic – peeled and chopped
6 slices	Prosciutto – sliced finely
2 cups (310g)	Fresh green peas (shelled)
4 cups (1 Litre)	Good chicken or vegetable stock
	Fresh basil leaves (a good handful)
5 tbls (100mL)	Cream
	Nutmeg
12	Rocket leaves – shredded
	Salt and pepper

In a heavy-based soup pot, heat the olive oil and sweat off the leek, zucchini and garlic for a couple of minutes.
Add the proscuitto and green peas.

Add in the stock and bring to the boil.

Simmer quickly for 5 minutes, adding the basil 1 minute from the end, and remove from heat. Allow it to cool a little before passing through a food processor.

Season well with nutmeg, salt and pepper.

Just before serving reheat the soup, adding the cream.

Serve garnished with shredded rocket leaves.

CHICKEN LAKSA
SERVES 4

FOR THE SOUP:

2 cups (500mL)	Chicken stock
2 cups (500mL)	Coconut milk
6	Deep-fried bean curd cakes
6	Chicken thighs – cut into strips
1 cup (90g)	Bean sprouts
2	Eggs – hard-boiled and halved
4	Green shallots – julienned
1 cup	Rice vermicelli – soaked in boiling water
1 tbls	Raw sugar
	Fish sauce to tast
3 tbls	Oil
2	Kaffir lime leaves
$^{1}/_{2}$ bunch	Coriander leaves – chopped

SPICE PASTE:

6	Eshalots – peeled
4 cloves	Garlic – peeled
4 cm piece	Fresh ginger – peeled
2 stalks	Lemon grass – bruised (white part only)
6	Macadamia nuts
3-4	Dried red chillies
1 tsp	Coriander
1 tsp	Cumin
1 tsp	Turmeric
1 tsp	Belacan (dried shrimp paste) (see Glossary, page 155)

To prepare the spice paste, in a food processor, work all the ingredients together to form a chunky paste.

In a large saucepan, heat half the oil and fry the spice paste till it is aromatic, about 5 minutes.

Then add the chicken stock and the coconut milk and bring to the boil.

Reduce heat and simmer gently, adding the sugar, lime leaves and fish sauce to taste.

In a large frying pan heat the remaining oil and sauté the chicken lightly before adding it to the soup to continue cooking.

To serve:
Place some drained, soaked vermicelli, bean sprouts, and shallots into the bottom of each bowl. Ladle in the soup and garnish with half a hard-boiled egg, chopped coriander and a bean curd cake.

For the lover of seafood laksa, substituting prawns, fish and fish stock for the chicken will prove simple and satisfying

sand

* Sandwich of Grilled Summer Vegetables with Pesto and Aioli
* Sandwich of Rare Roast Beef, Beetroot and Horseradish
* Sandwich of Prawns with Dill and Lemon Dressing
* Sandwich of BBQ pork, Cucumber and Snow Pea Sprouts with Sweet Chilli Sauce
* Sandwich of Chicken with Roasted Tomatoes and Basil Mayonnaise
* Sandwich of Baked Haloumi with Zucchini and Green Olives
* Hamburgers
* BBQ Tuna Burgers with Sweet Pickled Cucumber and Wasabi Cream
* Pumpkin, Basil and Sundried Tomato Burgers with Toasted Olive Bread
* Frittata with Potato and Asparagus
* Pies

wiches
burgers, frittata and pies

Most of us spent portions of our childhood unwrapping brown paper bags filled with dreary triangles of dull bread with even duller fillings. The legacy of the school sandwich is unfortunate; some of us have never recovered.

Whilst I'll admit that sandwiches can still go either way, the observation of a few simple rules can raise the lowly sandwich to its full potential as a satisfying meal.

Good, fresh bread is, of course, essential.

Be sure to choose the right bread for your fillings.

Avoid 'soggy bread syndrome' at all costs, keeping things like tomatoes and beetroot to the middle of the sandwich. Butter or mayonnaise on both sides of the sandwich will also help.

Big, deep fillings are fine if you are to eat your sandwich sitting down, but way too tricky for those on the move.

If it is to be eaten on the hop, avoid the 'trail of shredded lettuce syndrome'.

The following recipes are meant to serve as ideas that can be adapted to your own tastes and requirements.

SANDWICH OF GRILLED SUMMER VEGETABLES
WITH PESTO AND AIOLI

Selection of grilled vegetables, such as zucchini, red capsicum, eggplant, onion, kumara.
(Most good delis have a selection of grilled vegies)
Bread of your choice – baguette, wood-fired
Pesto (see Basics, page 151)
Aioli (see Basics, page 151)

Layer the grilled vegetables onto the bread and finish with a generous dollop each of pesto and aioli.

Prosciutto or finely sliced salmon may be added to the sandwich if you prefer.

SANDWICH OF RARE ROAST BEEF, BEETROOT AND HORSERADISH

	Rare roast beef – thinly sliced
	Bread of your choice – buttered
1	Fresh beetroot (small) – grated (cooked or raw, depending on your taste)
1 tbls	Horseradish
1 tbls	Sour cream
3/4 tbls	Capers – chopped
2	Green shallots – chopped finely
	Watercress or rocket, for garnish
	Pepper

In a bowl, combine the grated beetroot, capers, shallots, sour cream and horseradish. Season well.

Layer the beef between slices of the buttered bread, topped with the beetroot mixture and the watercress or rocket.

SANDWICH OF PRAWNS WITH DILL AND LEMON DRESSING

Peeled prawns

Bread of your choice (Baguettes preferable)

Watercress sprigs

Mayonnaise (see Basics, page 150)

Dill - chopped

Lemon zest

In a bowl combine the prawns, mayonnaise, chopped dill and lemon juice to taste.

Fill the buttered baguette with the prawn mixture and finish with some freshly picked watercress leaves.

SANDWICH OF BBQ PORK, CUCUMBER AND SNOW PEA SPROUTS WITH SWEET CHILLI SAUCE

Lebanese flat bread

Chinese BBQ pork (or duck), sliced

Spanish (red) onion – sliced very finely

Snow pea sprouts

Lebanese cucumbers – sliced finely with skin on

Sweet chilli sauce (bottled)

Lime juice

Sesame seeds

Fresh coriander leaves

Combine sliced BBQ pork, coriander, sesame seeds, Spanish onion, cucumber and snow pea sprouts with the sweet chilli sauce and lime juice. Spoon the filling into the lebanese bread and roll up.

Sandwich of Chicken with Roasted Tomatoes
and Basil Mayonnaise

Cooked chicken breast meat

Bread of your choice – buttered

Roasted Tomatoes

(see Basics, page 145)

Avocado – sliced

Good quality purchased or

Homemade Mayonnaise (see Basics,

page 150)

Basil leaves

Chop the basil leaves finely and mix into the mayonnaise.

Slice the chicken breast finely and layer onto the buttered bread with the roasted tomatoes and avocado. Finish with the basil mayonnaise.

Sandwich of Baked Haloumi
with Zucchini and Green Olives
SERVES 4

4	Lebanese bread pockets
2	Zucchini – sliced and grilled
125g	Haloumi cheese – crumbled
12	Green olives – pitted and chopped
4	Roma tomatoes – sliced
	Parsley (a handful) – chopped roughly
1 tsp	Rosemary – chopped finely
	Olive oil

Gently split the lebanese bread, taking great care not to tear it.

In a bowl, mix all the remaining ingredients except the olive oil and gently spoon some mixture into the cavity of each bread pocket, making sure that the mixture is evenly distributed throughout each pocket.

Brush both the top and the bottom of each sandwich with the olive oil and place onto a flat baking tray.

Cook the pockets in a fairly hot oven, turning them over once so that each side is golden brown and crispy.

Serve with a salad of rocket leaves and parmesan.

The possibilities for fillings are infinite, so please experiment to find your own personal creations.

burgers

HAMBURGERS

SERVES 6

750g	Beef mince (premium quality)
1	Brown onion (large) – chopped very finely
2 cloves	Garlic – minced finely
1	Egg
1 cup (80g)	Fresh breadcrumbs
1 tbls	Worcestershire sauce
2 tbls	Horseradish relish
1 tbls	Dijon mustard
2 tbls	Olive oil
	Tabasco sauce, to taste
	Salt and pepper

Mix all the ingredients together thoroughly.

Shape into 6 patties. Place on a plate and cover. Chill in the fridge till needed.

To cook the patties, heat a little olive oil in a non-stick frying pan over a medium flame.

Cook the patties for about 4 minutes on each side, according to your taste for rare, medium or well done.

Serve with any (or all!) of the following in a toasted burger bun:

* Cheese
* Beetroot
* Tomato Salsa (see Mick's Tomato Salsa, Basics, page 152)
* Grilled eggplant
* Grilled zucchini
* Caramelised Onion (see Basics, page 148)
* Roasted Capsicum (see Basics, page 147)
* Homemade chutney or pickle (see recipe for Zucchini Pickle, page 149, Spicy Tomato Chutney, page 149)
* Rocket
* Pesto (see Basics, page 151)
* Aioli (see Basics, page 151)
* Guacamole (see recipe page 145)
* Tzatziki (see recipe page 38)
* Hummus (see recipe page 39)

BBQ Tuna Burgers
with Sweet Pickled Cucumber
and Wasabi

Serves 6

Burgers:

400g	Fresh tuna – cubed
6	Green shallots (green part included) – chopped finely
1 cm piece	Ginger – grated
	Juice of 2 limes
2 tbls	Teriyaki sauce
2 tsp	Sesame oil
$^1/_2$ bunch	Coriander – chopped roughly

Pickled cucumber:

1	Telegraph cucumber (medium)
3 tbls	Mirin (rice wine)
2 tbls	White sugar
1 tsp	Sesame seeds
1	Birdseye chilli – de-seeded and finely chopped

Wasabi Cream:

1 tub (200g)	Sour cream
	Juice of 1 lime
2-3 tsp	Wasabi (see Glossary, page 155) – mixed with water to a paste
$^1/_2$ tsp	Sugar

Garnish:

	Peanut oil and olive oil, for cooking
12 slices	Italian wood-fired bread
1	Avocado (large)
2	Vine ripened tomatoes – sliced
$^1/_2$ punnet	Snow pea sprouts
	Fresh coriander leaves

To prepare the burgers:
In a food processor, pulse the tuna till it is a rough chop (not a puréed mass).

Transfer to a mixing bowl, add all the other ingredients and mix thoroughly.

Shape into 6 patties. Cover and refrigerate till needed.

To prepare the cucumber:
Run a vegetable peeler down the length of the cucumbers to produce long, fine 'ribbons'.

Mix the other ingredients and pour over the cucumbers.

Leave to stand for at least 10 minutes before using.

To prepare the wasabi cream:
Combine all the ingredients thoroughly, adjusting the quantity of wasabi to your preference - it is *very* hot.

To serve:
Heat your BBQ to a very high heat.

Brush the patties on both sides with a little peanut oil and cook on each side for roughly 1 minute, according to your taste.

Brush the slices of wood-fired bread with olive oil and lightly BBQ these.

Slice the avocado and place on top of half the bread slices, topping with the tomatoes, snow pea sprouts, tuna burgers and coriander leaves.

Finish with the pickled cucumber, wasabi cream and remaining bread slices.

PUMPKIN, BASIL AND SUN-DRIED TOMATO BURGERS
WITH TOASTED OLIVE BREAD
SERVES 6

12 slices	Olive bread – toasted
400g	Pumpkin – peeled, cooked and lightly mashed
1	Brown onion (large) – sliced finely
2 cloves	Garlic – chopped finely
8	Sun-dried tomatoes – chopped
1 tbls	Oil from the sun-dried tomatoes
$^2/_3$ cup (100g)	Pine nuts – toasted
125g	Tofu – mashed
$^1/_2$ cup (100g)	Ground almonds
1 cup	Breadcrumbs (preferably fresh)
20 leaves	Basil – chopped roughly
1	Egg – beaten lightly
	Olive oil, for frying
	Salt and pepper

FOR GARNISH:

(Any of the following)

Radish, rocket, roasted eggplant, roasted capsicum, Roasted Tomatoes (see Basics, page 147), Pesto (see Basics, page 151), Tapenade (see Basics, page 152), Aioli (see Basics, page 151), Spicy Tomato Salsa (see Basics, page 149), sweet mango chutney

In a frying pan, heat a little olive oil and sauté the onion and garlic till softened. Add the sun-dried tomatoes, their oil, and the pine nuts.

Transfer the onion mixture to a bowl, add the egg, pumpkin, mashed tofu, ground almonds, breadcrumbs, basil, salt and pepper and mix thoroughly. Shape into 6 patties, cover and refrigerate till needed.

The patties can be cooked in a non-stick frying pan, or on a tray in the oven, for about 5 minutes a side. The aim is to have them crisp and golden on the outside, warm and sweet on the inside. To serve, let your imagination run. I have listed just a few of the possible options to accompany these burgers.

Sweet potatoes can be used instead of pumpkin if you prefer.

Frittata with Potato
and Asparagus
Serves 6

6	Free-range eggs (large)
2	Potatoes (large) – boiled till soft, then cubed
1 bunch	Asparagus – cut into 2.5cm pieces and blanched
2	Onions – sliced thinly
2 cloves	Garlic – chopped finely
4 tbls	Parmesan cheese – grated
	Fresh parsley leaves (a handful) – chopped
	Fresh basil leaves (a handful) – chopped
6 tbls	Olive oil
	Salt and pepper

Variations

Frittata can be varied endlessly according to the content of your fridge, vegetable rack and imagination. Here are just a few suggestions:

* Mushrooms, leek and pine nuts
* Red capsicum, eggplant and sun-dried tomatoes
* Prosciutto, artichokes and onions
* Spinach, blue cheese and walnuts
* Zucchini, ham and sage
* Kumara, salami, rocket and olives
* Potatoes, peas and a touch of Indian curry paste

With a versatility born from the endless variations of fillings, frittata makes an excellent light meal with salad or as cold picnic fare.

Break the eggs into a bowl and whisk gently with a fork. Add the parmesan cheese and salt and pepper to taste.

In a large heavy-based frying pan, heat the olive oil and fry the onion, and garlic together. Once the onions have softened, add the potatoes, asparagus and herbs. The pan should be steaming hot by now so pour on the eggs and immediately turn down the heat.

Continue cooking till the underside is golden brown, (you can check this by lifting up the edge with a plastic spatula). When the bottom is cooked, the top can be finished off under the grill. Turn the frittata onto a plate.

pies

Pies have become an intrinsic part of Australian food culture. Hearty, warming and homely, the great winter staple has long since escaped its obligatory filling of beef and gravy, and is now home to almost as many different fillings as there are toppings to the modern day pizza. Whilst a great deal of imagination and creativity can be found beneath the crisp, golden layer of pastry, pies are not always what they seem since they can also provide an excellent way of breathing new life into all manner of leftovers.

There are some good quality pastries available commercially, puff and filo being the obvious two, but I would suggest that when it comes to shortcrust or sweet pastry it is well worth the time and effort to make your own, (see Basics, page 154). Pies, tortes and bakes are extremely versatile and lend themselves well to preparation in advance. Throughout the book I give many variations, from Andrew's Tuscan Spinach Pie, using a parmesan and breadcrumb pastry, to the exotic Chicken B'stilla. Listed below are some more suggestions but, as with the sandwich and the frittata, you are only limited by your imagination.

63

* Braised beef with red wine, mushrooms and walnuts, with a mashed potato and parsnip topping.
* Chicken, celery, haricot beans and roasted garlic, with puff pastry.
* Spinach, beetroot, fetta and ricotta, with filo pastry.
* Slow-cooked lamb shoulder with borlotti beans and sage, with puff pastry.
* Seafood marinara with white wine and cream, topped with a potato and horseradish mash.
* Sausage with roasted sweet potatoes, red capsicum and basil, with puff pastry.
* Chicken, leek, roasted tomatoes and caramelised onions, with filo pastry.
* Eggplant, zucchini and potatoes with roasted cashews and Moroccan spices (cumin, cinnamon, coriander and turmeric) with filo pastry.
* Smoked trout, fennel and leeks with dill and lemon zest with puff pastry.

salads

* Potted Tuna and Potatoes with Snake Bean Salad and Balsamic Dressing
* Caesar Salad
* Salad of Braised Artichokes, Sun-dried Tomatoes and Olives
* Korean Beef Salad
* Baked Ricotta and Pumpkin Salad
* Tomato, Bocconcini and Avocado Salad with Basil and Parmesan Dressing
* Thai Chicken Salad with Lime, Coconut and Coriander
* Grilled Chicken Thighs with Tabouli and Eggplant Relish
* Tomato Timbales with Grilled Sardines
* Warm Japanese Chicken and Sesame Salad
* Pappadum Stacks with Oysters and Smoked Eggplant
* Vine Ripened Tomatoes with Ricotta, Tapenade and Walnut Biscotti

Potted Tuna and Potatoes with Snake Bean Salad
and Balsamic Dressing
Serves 6

500g	Waxy potatoes - boiled and mashed (see Basics, page 145)
600g	Cooked and flaked tuna (tinned will do, fresh is better)
3	Green shallots – finely chopped
2 sticks	Celery – finely chopped
2 tbls	Capers – finely chopped
1 cup	Mayonnaise (see Basics, page 150)
$^1/_2$ bunch	Parsley – chopped
	Pinch of nutmeg
	Salt and pepper

For the Snake Bean Salad:

1 bunch	Snake beans – blanched and refreshed
6	Eggs – hard-boiled
6	Roma tomatoes
1	Telegraph cucumber
1 bunch	Rocket or watercress
24	Black olives
18	Basil leaves
1	Quantity Balsamic Dressing (see Basics, page 150)

In a large bowl, combine all the above ingredients, mix well and season to taste. Make sure that when you add the mayonnaise the mixture doesn't become too thin and runny, this will depend on the potatoes and the thickness of the mayonnaise.

Spoon this mixture either into 6 individual dariole moulds or one loaf tin or mould.

Cover with plastic wrap and refrigerate for at least four hours before unmoulding.

To serve:
Make the salad using all the ingredients, dress lightly with the Balsamic Dressing and serve with the unmoulded tuna and wood-fired toast.

Caesar Salad
Serves 4

4	Baby cos lettuce (or 2 normal size)
8	Anchovy fillets
4 rashers	Bacon – grilled till crispy and chopped
4 heaped tbls	Garlic croutes (see Basics, page 149)
1 quantity	Caesar Dressing (see Basics, page 151)
100g piece	Parmesan – shaved

Wash the baby cos thoroughly, you should be able to use all the leaves.

Dry the leaves and place in a large mixing bowl, tearing them gently if they are too big.

Sprinkle with the bacon, croutons and anchovies, tossing carefully.

Divide among 4 salad bowls or plates and finish with the dressing and shaved parmesan.

SALAD OF BRAISED ARTICHOKES,
SUN-DRIED TOMATOES AND OLIVES
SERVES 6

6	Artichokes
1	Onion – chopped roughly
1	Carrot – chopped roughly
1 stick	Celery – chopped roughly
4	Sun-dried tomatoes
24	Kalamata olives
4 cloves	Garlic – chopped
$^1/_2$ bunch	Parsley – chopped
$^1/_2$ bunch	Chives – chopped
	Olive oil to cover
2 tbls	Raspberry vinegar
	Juice of one lemon plus a half
2-3	Bay leaves
2 sprigs	Thyme
	Salt and pepper

To prepare the artichokes, pull off all the outer green leaves and discard. Cut off the top half of the globe and trim the stalk. Place immediately into acidulated water to avoid oxidation.

In a stainless steel saucepan, place the carrot, celery, onion, bay leaves, and thyme. Cover deeply with water and bring to the boil.

When boiling, add the artichokes, half a lemon and enough olive oil to just cover the surface of the water and place a plate on top to push the artichokes below the surface. Bring back to the boil, reduce the heat and simmer gently till cooked, 15–20 minutes.

Allow to cool in the water, then cut into quarters and place in a bowl. Add the garlic, herbs and lemon.

Dress liberally with 6–8 tablespoons olive oil and the vinegar, seasoning well. Serve with the olives and sun-dried tomatoes.

Whilst the raspberry vinaigrette brings a very distinctive flavour to the artichokes, balsamic vinegar can be used in its place.

KOREAN BEEF SALAD
SERVES 6

1kg	Rump piece – marinated in soy, ginger, sesame oil, black pepper and garlic.
1 packet (250g)	Rice vermicelli – softened in boiling water
1	Red capsicum – julienned finely
2	Carrots – julienned
2 sticks	Celery – julienned
500g	Green beans – put through slicer
2 tbls	Toasted sesame seeds
	Chilli (to taste) – chopped
3	Green shallots – sliced finely (diagonally)
	Korean Dressing (see Basics, page 153)

Marinate the whole piece of rump, preferably overnight, but for at least 3 hours.

Preheat the oven to 220°C. Roast the beef for 20 minutes. It should be very rare. The meat should be rested well and then sliced very finely.

Combine the vegetables with the softened, drained rice noodles and mix well with the Korean Dressing.

Place on individual plates and mound with the beef.

Garnish with some toasted sesame seeds, chopped chilli and green shallots.

BAKED RICOTTA
AND PUMPKIN SALAD

SERVES 6

1kg	Ricotta
1–2 cloves	Garlic – peeled
2	Capsicum (red)
500g	Pumpkin – cleaned and cut into pieces
1 bunch	Rocket
500g	Green beans or snake beans – blanched
1 cup (100g)	Grated parmesan
1 sprig	Fresh rosemary – chopped
1 sprig	Fresh thyme – chopped
	Generous amounts of pitted black olives
	Salt and pepper
	Horseradish Vinaigrette, (see Basics, page 150)
	Parmesan shavings, for garnish

Preheat the oven to 190°C.

To bake the ricotta, in a bowl, combine the ricotta with the parmesan, chopped herbs and salt and pepper to taste.

Pour into well-oiled ovenproof baking dish and bake for 40 minutes.

Remove from the oven and allow to cool till the ricotta starts to become firm before turning out onto a serving dish.

Roast the capsicum, seed and skin (see Basics, page 147). Slice into lengths.

Roast the pumpkin with the addition of some whole garlic cloves, and some extra thyme and rosemary if preferred. Allow to cool.

To assemble:
Place the rocket, capsicum, olives, pumpkin and beans in a bowl and toss generously with the Horseradish Vinaigrette.

Arrange attractively on a large serving dish that has the sliced ricotta on it. Garnish with shaved parmesan.

Serve with Walnut Biscotti (see Basics, page 154).

Baked ricotta can be served either warm or cool (i.e., room temperature). It is much easier to handle and slice when cool. If you like your ricotta more 'cheesy' you can add some parmesan, blue cheese or any other cheese of your choice before cooking.

TOMATO, BOCCONCINI AND AVOCADO SALAD
WITH BASIL AND PARMESAN DRESSING
SERVES 4

4	Perfectly ripe tomatoes – sliced
2	Avocados - sliced
2 bunches (300g)	Baby rocket – picked and washed
8	Fresh baby bocconcini – sliced
16	Black olives
150g	Green beans – trimmed and blanched
	(asparagus can be substituted)
	Parmesan shavings – for garnish
	Salt and pepper
	BASIL AND PARMESAN DRESSING:
1 cup (250mL)	Plain Vinaigrette
	(see Basics, page 150)
2 tbls	Pesto (see Basics, page 151)

To prepare the dressing, combine the vinaigrette and the pesto. In a bowl, toss the rocket and green beans together. Dress generously with the dressing and season with salt and pepper to taste.

To assemble, arrange the tomatoes, bocconcini and avocados attractively around 4 serving plates. Arrange the rocket and beans in the centre, scatter with the olives and finish with parmesan shavings.

Serve with garlic bruschetta or a slice of olive bread, such as the one used in the Roasted Tomato and Olive Tart (see Basics, page 154).

This is a really simple, yet satisfying, summer lunch dish. The pesto dressing gives the whole thing a delicious lift.

THAI CHICKEN SALAD
WITH LIME, COCONUT AND CORIANDER
SERVES 6

12	Chicken thigh fillets
2	Carrots
1	Telegraph cucumber
100g	Bean sprouts
100g	Snow pea sprouts
4	Kaffir lime leaves – finely shredded
1 bunch	Coriander – pick leaves and retain stalks for dressing
15	Mint leaves
$1/2$	Coconut – shaved and toasted, (see Basics, page 148)
$2/3$ cup (100g)	Roasted peanuts
	Thai Dressing, (see Basics, page 152)

For the salad:
Shave the carrots and cucumber lengthways into long strips using a vegetable peeler and place in a large bowl with the sprouts, shredded lime leaves, coriander leaves and mint leaves.

Toss gently with the shaved coconut and peanuts.

Grill the chicken thighs until the skin is golden and crispy, slice and add to the salad.

Toss well with the Thai Dressing and serve immediately.

Another Thomas Street Café favourite, this works every bit as well with BBQ octopus.

GRILLED CHICKEN THIGHS
WITH TABOULI AND EGGPLANT RELISH
SERVES 6

MARINADE:

9	Chicken thigh steaks (large) – skin on
2 cloves	Garlic – chopped
	Lemon zest
	Olive oil
	Salt and pepper

TABOULI:

1 bunch	Flat leaf parsley – chopped roughly
$^1/_2$ bunch	Fresh mint – chopped roughly
2	Lebanese cucumbers (small) – diced with the skin on
6	Green shallots – chopped finely, including the green part
$^1/_2$ cup (85g)	Cracked wheat (burghul)
3	Ripe tomatoes – chopped
	Juice of 2 lemons
4 tbls	Olive oil
	Salt and pepper

EGGPLANT RELISH:

1	Eggplant (large)
1	Spanish (red) onion – chopped finely
2 cloves	Garlic – chopped finely
$^1/_2$ bunch	Coriander
1 tsp	Ground cumin
1 tsp	Ground coriander
1 $^1/_2$ tbls	Ketjap manis (Indonesian sweet soy)
1 tblsb	Balsamic vinegar
2 tbls	Pine nuts – toasted
	Olive oil

Marinate the chicken thighs for at least one hour before cooking.

Rinse the cracked wheat thoroughly under cold water and then soak in hot water for 25 minutes.

Drain the wheat well and pat dry with paper towel to absorb any excess moisture. Place into a mixing bowl with all the other tabouli ingredients apart from the tomatoes, lemon juice, and olive oil. These should be added just 10 minutes before you serve the salad.

For the eggplant relish:

Cut the eggplant in half lengthways and then finely slice into half moons.

Place in a colander and sprinkle with salt—leave for 30 minutes. Rinse the eggplant well and pat dry to remove excess moisture.

In a large heavy based frying pan, heat some olive oil and fry the eggplant till crisp and golden on both sides. They will absorb quite a lot of olive oil so be prepared for this.

Once the eggplant is cooked, place into a bowl.

Heat a little more oil and sauté the onion and garlic till tender. Add to the eggplant along with all the other ingredients. Mix through well and serve this on top of the hot grilled chicken.

To serve:
Cook the chicken either on the BBQ or under the grill, so that the skin becomes golden and crisp, allowing 1$^1/_2$ thighs per person.

Serve with the tabouli, the eggplant relish and, if desired, a tablespoon of plain yoghurt on each plate.

The relish can be served either warm or cold, depending on your taste.

Tabouli just oozes good health to me and is so simple to prepare. The eggplant relish is best prepared in advance so that the flavours can mingle. But the most important thing is not to drown the salad in too much dressing or to add it too early.

TOMATO TIMBALES
WITH GRILLED SARDINES
SERVES 6

1	Stale loaf – Italian wood-fired bread
6	Vine ripened tomatoes (large)
18	Sardine fillets
2	Roasted red capsicum – skinned and seeded (see Basics, page 151)
2 cloves	Garlic – minced
1 tbls	Capers – chopped
18	Kalamata olives – pitted and chopped
2 tbls	Sherry vinegar (white wine can be substituted)
1 bunch	Baby rocket leaves
$^1/_2$ bunch	Basil leaves
	Juice of $^1/_2$ lemon
	Salt and pepper
	Extra virgin olive oil
6	Dariole moulds

Slice the bread thinly.

Blanch the tomatoes peel and seed them over a sieve placed in a bowl to reserve all the juices. Skin and seed the capsicum over the same bowl. Add the garlic, vinegar and 3 tablespoons of olive oil to the juices and season to taste with salt and pepper.

Chop the tomatoes and capsicum roughly and mix with the basil, olives and capers.

Pass each slice of bread through the tomato juice mixture and completely line each of 6 dariole moulds with the softened bread.

Pack each cavity with the tomato mixture and press down firmly, so there are no air pockets left.

Spoon over any remaining tomato juice and cover with another layer of softened bread.

Cover the moulds with plastic wrap and refrigerate for at least three hours before serving.

On a flat baking tray, lay out the sardines, skin side up, and brush with olive oil and lemon juice. Place under a hot grill for $1^1/_2$ minutes or until cooked.

To serve:
Gently run a knife around each mould and turn out onto a bed of rocket and grilled sardines.

With success depending on the sweetness and ripeness of the tomatoes, this 'tomato summer pudding' is a great way to use up stale bread. This dish was inspired by those brilliant 'fat ladies' of BBC fame with the sardines filling it out to become a full and satisfying lunch.

WARM JAPANESE CHICKEN
AND SESAME SALAD
SERVES 4

4	Chicken breasts (off the bone)
200g	Baby spinach – washed
1	Spanish (red) onion (small) – very thinly sliced
2 tbls	Sesame seeds
1 bulb	Witloof (Belgium endive) – shredded finely
2 cloves	Garlic – peeled
1	Carrot (large) – julienned
	Peanut oil and sesame oil, extra
12	Fresh basil leaves – for garnish
	Gomasio (see Glossary, page 155) (optional)

FOR THE DRESSING:

$^1/_4$ bunch	Coriander
1 tbls	Sugar
2 tbls	Soy Sauce
3 tsp	Mirin
$^1/_2$ cup (125mL)	Tahini
	Juice of $1^1/_2$ lemons
70mL	Peanut oil
3 tsp	Sesame oil

To make the dressing, place all the ingredients in a blender or food processor, except the oils, and process until combined. With the machine running slowly drizzle in the peanut and sesame oils. Set to one side.

For the salad:
Brush each chicken breast with some extra peanut oil and place on a very hot grill pan or BBQ.

Cook evenly for 4 minutes on each side, or until cooked through. Set to one side.

Heat 1 teaspoon sesame oil and $^1/_2$ tablespoon peanut oil in a wok. Throw in the garlic and when it is golden brown, add the washed spinach and literally stir around once, just enough to barely wilt the spinach.

Remove from the heat and add the carrot, spanish onion, and sesame seeds.

Add $^1/_2$ the dressing and toss through gently.

To serve:
Slice the chicken and place it in a bowl, add the remaining dressing and toss well.

Place the spinach on the base of each plate. Arrange the chicken on top. Sprinkle with some gomasio, shredded endive and the basil leaves.

PAPPADUM STACKS
WITH OYSTERS AND SMOKED EGGPLANT

SERVES 4

12	Pappadums – cooked
32	Prawns – shelled
32	Oysters (fresh)
1	Telegraph cucumber – de-seeded, peeled and chopped finely
2 sticks	Celery – chopped finely
2	Green shallots – chopped finely
1	Nashi apple – peeled and chopped finely
2 tbls	Vinaigrette (see Basics, page 150)
12 tbls	Babaghanoush (see recipe, page 42)
8 tsp	Mayonnaise (see Basics, page 150)
	Salt and pepper

In a bowl, combine the celery, cucumber, shallots and apple. Mix with the vinaigrette and season with salt and pepper.

To assemble:
Place a spoonful of Babaghanoush on the base of each of 4 plates and place a pappadum on top.

Now put a spoonful of the salad, 4 prawns and 4 oysters on each pappadum, finishing with a dollop of mayonnaise.

Lay out 4 other pappadums. Put on a dollop of Babaghanoush and repeat this process with the salad and seafood before lifting them with an egg slice and placing them gently on the first layer.

Finish the stack with a third pappadum.

Serve with a bitter green salad such as endive or Belgian witloof.

The smoked eggplant of the Babaghanoush sits wonderfully with the freshness of the salad and the saltiness of the seafood. An excellent and easily prepared entrée or light lunch.

Salads

75

VINE RIPENED TOMATOES
WITH RICOTTA, TAPENADE AND WALNUT BISCOTTI
SERVES 6

6	Perfectly ripe tomatoes
	(large – or 12 small)
2 tbls	Olive oil
1 tbls	Balsamic vinegar
	Salt and pepper
1	Telegraph cucumber
1 bunch (150g)	Rocket leaves
2	Avocados – sliced
250g	Ricotta
1	Quantity Tapenade
	(see Basics, page 152)
12	Walnut Biscotti
	(see Basics, page 154)

Blanch the tomatoes, refresh under cold water and remove the skins.

Cut the top off each tomato and carefully remove the seeds. Reserve the seeds.

Season the tomatoes well and invert them on a plate. Refrigerate till needed.

Pass the tomato pulp through a sieve, and mix the liquid with the olive oil and balsamic vinegar.

With a vegetable peeler, run down the side of the cucumber to remove the peel, and then continue, producing long ribbons of cucumber flesh.

To assemble:
Wash and trim the rocket and place attractively on separate plates with the avocado slices and cucumber strips.

Spoon the ricotta into the cavities of the tomatoes and top with a generous dollop of the Tapenade.

Finish with the tomato balsamic dressing and serve with the Walnut Biscotti.

An attractive summer salad, the sweetness of the Walnut Biscotti provides the perfect foil for the tomatoes and olives. A tapenade of green olives will work just as well.

vegies

MILLE-FEUILLE OF PROSCIUTTO, ZUCCHINI AND MASCARPONE

SERVES 4

100g	Prosciutto
1 bunch	Rocket – picked from stalks
1	Lebanese cucumber – diced
500g	Zucchini
2	Green shallots – chopped
1	Red capsicum – roasted, skinned and seeded (see Basics, page 147)
1 tub (250g)	Mascarpone
2 tbls	Mayonnaise
$^1/_2$ tbls	Dijon mustard
8	Fresh basil leaves – torn
	Puff pastry – 2 pre-rolled sheets, thawed
	Olive oil – for frying
	Salt and pepper
	Milk – for glazing

Slice the zucchini thinly, lengthways, and fry in olive oil till soft, tender and golden brown on each side. Set to one side.

In a mixing bowl, combine the cucumber, green shallots, rocket, basil and thinly sliced red capsicum. Season with salt and pepper.

In a small bowl, combine the mayonnaise and mustard and fold this into the rocket mix.

Preheat the oven to 200°C. Trim the edges of the puff pastry and cut each sheet into 2 rectangles. You will need 3 of these. Place on baking trays, brush with milk and bake till golden brown on the top. Remove from the oven and allow to cool slightly.

To assemble:
On two of the rectangles of puff pastry, spread the mascarpone generously and lay the zucchini and prosciutto evenly across.

Top with the rocket mixture and gently layer one rectangle on top of the other.

Finish with the final rectangle of puff pastry, slice into four and serve.

* Millefeuille of Proscuitto, Zucchini and Marscapone
* Medley of Roasted Summer Vegetables with Pesto and Aioli
* Andrew's Tuscan Spinach Pie
* Roulade of Eggplant, Capsicum and Goat's Cheese
* Quesadilla with Kumera, Spanish Onion and Peanuts with
  Guacamole and Tomato Salsa
* Roasted Banana Chillies with Ricotta and Sun-Dried Tomatoes
* Roasted Tomato and Olive Tart
* Gado Gado
* Twice Baked Potatoes with Asparagus, Mushrooms, and Parmesan
* Parsnip and Parmesan Loaf Served with a Fennel and Olive Medley
* Vegetable Torte with Pumpkin and Couscous Pastry

vegies

79

Medley of Roasted Summer Vegetables
with Pesto and Aioli

Roma tomatoes – halved lengthways

Pumpkin – peeled and cut into pieces

Squash (yellow or green) – cut in half

Beans – blanched and refreshed

Zucchini – halved lengthways

Corn – on the cob, cut into pieces

Pickling onions (small)

Red capsicums – quartered and seeded

Baby eggplants – halved lengthways

Garlic cloves

Basil leaves

– any roasting vegetable of your choice

Parsnip chips for garnish (optional)

Oil for deep-frying

MEDLEY JUICE:

1 cup	Water
2 tbls	Ketjap manis (Indonesian sweet soy)
	Juice from roasted vegetables
	Pesto
	(see Basics, page 151, for serving)
	Aioli
	(see Basics, page 151, for serving)

Preheat the oven to 200°C.

Roast the vegetables — blanch any such as, e.g. corn or beans.

Assemble the vegetables generously on a large serving dish and keep warm.

Place the roasting tin over direct heat, add the water and ketjap manis, reduce the medley juices stirring to mix in all the browned and glazed bits from the pan. Add the basil leaves at the last moment.

Pour the reduction over the vegetables and serve immediately with bowls of Pesto and Aioli.

To make the Parsnip Chips:
Using a vegetable peeler, peel long strips off parsnips.

Deep fry in small batches and drain well on absorbent paper.

Place these on top of the vegetables just before serving.

This remarkably simple dish was a runaway success at Thomas Street Cafe.

vegies

81

ANDREW'S TUSCAN SPINACH PIE

SERVES 6

2 bunches	(about 2kg) Silverbeet – stripped, washed, blanched and squeezed to remove excess water
2	Onions – sliced
6-8 cloves	Garlic – crushed
1/2 bunch	Thyme
1/2 bunch	Sage
1 tbls	Rosemary
1	Lemon – use the grated zest
	Sultanas
	Pine nuts – toasted
3 tbls	Cream
1 cup	Parmesan – grated
1 tbls	Butter
	Olive oil
	Salt and pepper

PIE CRUST:

$2^{1}/_{2}$ cups (250g)	Toasted breadcrumbs
$2^{1}/_{2}$ cups (250g)	Parmesan – grated
2 tbls	Rosemary leaves
$1^{1}/_{4}$ cups (300mL)	Olive oil

In a large frying pan, heat 2 tablespoons olive oil and sauté the garlic, onions, thyme, sage and rosemary.

Add the silverbeet, lemon zest, sultanas and toasted pine nuts and cook over a moderate heat for a few minutes.

Add the cream, and then the parmesan, and cook for one more minute.

Remove from heat. The mixture should be moist, but not at all runny.

Season well with salt and pepper.

To make the crust:
Preheat the oven to 180°C.

Combine the breadcrumbs, parmesan, rosemary and olive oil in a large bowl.

To assemble:
Press the crumb mixture into a buttered 25cm springform tin, making sure that it is evenly distributed, about 1.5cm thick and reaches right up the sides. It needs to be thick enough to hold the filling, but not so thick that it is too crusty when cooked. Press the sides well.

Fill the crust with the spinach mixture, pressing it in firmly.

Cover the top with more crust.

Place on a flat baking tray and bake on the middle shelf of the oven for 25–30 minutes.

Allow to cool slightly before cutting.

Serve with a green leaf salad, with sun-dried tomatoes, toasted pine nuts and shaved parmesan.

Variations:
* Add chopped sun-dried tomatoes to the spinach mix

* Add Roasted Tomatoes to the spinach mix (see Basics, page 145)

* Ricotta instead of cream

* Roasted pumpkin and red capsicum

Good friend and colleague Andrew Towns introduced this recipe to Thomas Street Cafe where it promptly went on the bestsellers list. The crust is so simple to prepare and can hold almost any filling that is not too moist. Leftovers will freeze very well.

ROULADE OF EGGPLANT,
CAPSICUM AND GOAT'S CHEESE
SERVES 6

2	Eggplant (approximately)
3	Red capsicums
200g	Goat's cheese – white Castello can be substituted
3 tbls	Cream
3 cloves	Garlic – unpeeled
10	Basil leaves
1 bunch	chives – chopped finely
	Olive oil – for grilling and roasting
	Salt and pepper

Preheat the oven to 200°C.

Place capsicums on a baking tray with the whole cloves of garlic. Drizzle with oil and bake for 30–40 minutes, turning frequently to prevent burning.

When fully roasted, remove from oven and place in a bowl, covering with plastic wrap. This step helps steam off the skin.

When cool enough to handle, remove the seeds, keeping the flesh in as large pieces as possible.

Keep any liquid from the capsicums to use as dressing for a rocket salad accompaniment.

Slice the eggplant thinly, lengthways. Salt and leave for 20 minutes before rinsing and patting dry.

Place the goat's cheese into a bowl and mash with a fork, slowly incorporating the cream. You may need to vary the amount of cream according to the softness of the goat's cheese. The mixture should be moist, but not at all runny, just firm enough to hold its own shape. Add the chopped herbs and season with salt and pepper.

Grill the eggplant slices till brown and softened and allow to cool in a tray. If you do not have a grill plate, use a frying pan, ensuring

sufficient oil to avoid dry frying. Eggplants absorb a lot of oil when cooking—their 'thirst' needs to be thoroughly catered for with this particular dish.

To assemble:
Lay out aluminium foil, shiny surface upward. Brush lightly with olive oil and season with salt and pepper.

Overlap the slices of eggplant to form a long oblong shape, ensuring there are no gaps.

Now lay the capsicum pieces on top of the eggplant, again with no gaps.

With a dessert spoon, gently place the goat's cheese about 5cm in from the long edge closest to you. Distribute the cheese evenly, the end result resembling a long sausage of goat's cheese.

With your fingers, bring the lower edges of eggplant up over the cheese, you can do this by gently rolling the foil over the sausage. Then bring the foil back towards you and gently begin to roll the roulade up. You will need to keep adjusting the tightness.

Once you have a long 'sausage roll', roll the foil around the roulade and gently, but firmly, correct the shape and twist the ends closed.

Lay on a flat tray in the fridge and leave for at least 2 hours.

To serve, slice the roulade and serve with rocket tossed with the capsicum oil, a touch of balsamic and crisp croutes on the side.

The Secret
This is not half as hard to make as it reads on paper or, indeed, looks on the plate.

Your guests, however, don't know that, and the spiraling folds of eggplant, capsicum and cheese do look pretty spectacular.

vegies

85

ROASTED BANANA CHILLIES
WITH RICOTTA AND SUN-DRIED TOMATOES
SERVES 4

12	Banana chillies
500g	Fresh ricotta
50g	Parmesan – grated
2	Green shallots – sliced finely
6	Sun-dried tomatoes – chopped finely
12	Basil leaves – chopped
2 tbls	Parsley – chopped
1 tbls	Toasted pine nuts
	Salt and pepper
	Olive oil

Preheat the oven to 180°C.

Place the banana chillies in a large bowl, cover in boiling water and set to one side for 3–4 minutes to soften the flesh slightly. Refresh under cold water. Drain and pat dry.

With a sharp knife, make a slit along the sides of the chillies, gently removing the seeds with your fingers, and rinsing under cold water to remove any remaining seeds.

Mix all the other ingredients except the olive oil together in a large mixing bowl. Season well with salt and pepper.

With a small teaspoon, gently fill each cavity with the ricotta mixture.

Place the chillies, slit side upwards, onto a baking tray, drizzle with olive oil and bake for 30 minutes.

Delicious served either warm or cold, with a crisp salad and extra parmesan if preferred.

Banana chillies come into their own when roasted this way— softening and caramelising slightly with the olive oil. Ideal for an antipasto plate.

ROASTED TOMATO
AND OLIVE TART
SERVES 4

FOR THE TART:

8	Roma tomatoes
2	Onions – sliced finely into half moons
2 sprigs	Fresh thyme – leaves only
2 tbls	Balsamic vinegar
3 tbls	Raw sugar
60g	Butter
	Salt and pepper
	Extra virgin olive oil
100g piece	Parmesan – shaved
	For the bread base (See recipe for Olive and Rosemary Bread, Basics, page 154)

Preheat the oven to 220°C.

Slice the tomatoes in half lengthways, place on an oiled baking tray and sprinkle with salt and pepper. Drizzle with olive oil and $1\frac{1}{2}$ tablespoons raw sugar. Roast these in the oven for 15 minutes. Set to one side. Reduce the oven temprature to 200°C.

Melt the butter in a heavy–based saucepan and add 1 tablespoon of olive oil.

Add the onion and thyme and cook over a moderate heat for 20 minutes, before adding the rest of the sugar and the balsamic vinegar. Continue cooking till the onions have caramelised. Set to one side and cool slightly.

To assemble:
Divide the olive bread dough into four pieces, roll out each and cut into a round to fit 4 (10cm) tart cases.

Place the rounds onto a lightly oiled baking tray, brush with olive oil and bake at 200°C for 12 minutes. Remove from the oven and set to one side.

Arrange the tomatoes in the base of each case and then top with the caramelised onion mixture.

Now place the olive bread on top, making sure that the bottom side of the bread is now uppermost.

Place the tart cases onto the flat baking tray and bake for a further 10 minutes.

Remove from the oven and let the tarts stand for about 5 minutes before inverting them onto plates.

Serve with shaved parmesan and a crisp green salad.

Quesadillas with
Kumara, Spanish Onion and Peanuts
with Guacamole and Tomato Salsa

Serves 6

6	Tortillas
1kg	Kumara – peeled, cubed and roasted
2	Spanish (red) onions – sliced finely in half moons
2 cloves	Garlic – minced
4	green shallots – chopped finely
2 cups (250g)	Cheddar
$\frac{1}{3}$ cup (60g)	Peanuts – toasted
$\frac{1}{2}$ bunch	Coriander – chopped
1	Red capsicum – sliced
1 tblsp	Olive oil
	Chilli to taste (optional)
	Vegetable oil
	Salt and pepper
1 quantity	Guacamole (See Basics, page 145)
1 quantity	Mick's Spicy Tomato Salsa (see Basics, page 149)
1 tub (300g)	Sour cream
	Coriander, shallots and chilli, for garnish

To make the filling:
In a frying pan heat the oil and sauté the onions, garlic, and chilli till the onions are slightly caramelised.

Add the red capsicum and cook for a further 5 minutes, turning the mixture frequently to avoid any burning.

In a large bowl, combine the roasted kumara, the onion mixture, green shallots, peanuts, cheese and coriander. Season well.

Preheat the oven to 200ºC.

To assemble:
Lay the tortillas flat on the bench.

Divide the filling mixture evenly, placing it across one half of each tortilla, leaving a 1cm border around the edge.

Fold the other half across the mixture so that you have a half moon effect.

Brush both sides of the tortilla very well with vegetable oil and place on a baking tray in the oven for about 5 minutes on each side.

The tortilla should be very crispy and golden on the outside with the cheese deliciously melted on the inside.

To serve:
Top each quesadilla with generous spoonfuls of guacamole and tomato salsa. Finish with some sour cream and a garnish of chopped chilli, shallots and fresh coriander.

GADO GADO
SERVES 6

3	Potatoes (large)
$^1/_2$	Cabbage (small)
2	Carrots (large)
500g	Green beans
250g	Snow peas
1	Telegraph cucumber
250g	Bean sprouts
6	Deep-fried tofu cakes (available from Asian food stores)
3	Eggs – hard-boiled, sliced
1 packet (50g)	Krupuk (prawn crackers, see Glossary, page 155)
6 serves	Jasmine rice – boiled

SATAY SAUCE:

1 cup (250g)	Peanut butter (crunchy)
1 cup (250mL)	Coconut milk
1	Onion (large) – chopped finely
3 cloves	Garlic – minced
2cm piece	Ginger – chopped finely
2cm piece	Lemon grass – chopped finely
1 tsp	Ground cumin
1 tbls	Ketjap manis (Indonesian sweet soy)
$^1/_2$ tsp	Red chilli (small) – chopped
	Water
	Juice of 1 lemon
1 tbls	Vegetable oil

Peel the potatoes and boil them in salted water till soft. Refresh under cold water and set to one side.

In a large saucepan bring water to the boil with some salt and quickly blanch all the other vegetables that require it (cabbage, carrots, green beans and snow peas). Refresh them in cold water. Alternatively, these vegetables can be steamed.

The vegetables are served at room temperature with the hot peanut sauce and boiled rice.

To make the satay sauce:
Heat the oil in a heavy – based saucepan. Add the onion, garlic, ginger, chilli, cumin, and lemon grass and cook gently for about 5 minutes. The onion and garlic should be slightly caramelised.

Fold in the peanut butter and quickly add $1–1^1/_2$ cups water and coconut milk, stirring to a smooth consistency.

Finish with the lemon juice and ketjap manis.

To serve:
Arrange the cooked vegetables with the cucumber, bean sprouts and tofu on a platter and finish with the hot satay sauce.

Garnish with the sliced boiled eggs and krupuk. Serve with boiled rice.

Healthy vegetables provide the perfect excuse for eating satay sauce!

TWICE BAKED POTATOES
WITH ASPARAGUS, MUSHROOMS AND PARMESAN
SERVES 4

4	Baking potatoes
	(Pontiacs or Sebagoare best)
1 bunch	Asparagus – chopped into 2.5cm
	pieces and blanched
$^2/_3$ cup (60g)	Parmesan – freshly grated
3 – 4 tbls (60–75mL)	Cream
1	Onion – sliced finely
1 clove	Garlic – minced
$^1/_2$ bunch	Chives – chopped
2 tbls	Olive oil
4	Flat mushrooms – sliced
1 stick	Celery – sliced thinly
	Olive oil
	Salt and pepper

Preheat the oven to 200°C.

Wash the potatoes thoroughly, pierce the skin and flesh with a sharp knife (once only), place on a baking tray and bake till soft, 45–60 minutes.

Remove from the oven and allow to cool completely.

In olive oil, sweat the onion and garlic till softened, add the mushrooms and celery and cook quickly for a couple of minutes. Remove from heat and set to one side.

Cut off the top section of each potato, leaving at least two thirds for the base.

Scoop out the insides but leave some potato around the insides to make a shell.

Place the scooped potato into a bowl and mix with the asparagus, mushroom mixture, chives, 2 tablespoons of olive oil, the cream and three quarters of the parmesan cheese. Season well with salt and pepper.

Fill each of the emptied potatoes with the filling and place back on a baking tray. Drizzle over some extra olive oil and bake for a further 15 minutes. Serve with the remaining parmesan cheese and a crisp green salad.

Variations:
* Artichokes, sun-dried tomatoes, pine nuts and basil

* Sweet corn, capsicum, fresh peas, garlic chives and ham

* Flaked tuna, green shallots, lemon zest and green olives

* Smoked salmon and dill, finished with salmon roe and mascarpone

* Chicken, toasted almonds, blue cheese and wilted spinach

There are as many fillings for these potatoes as there are cooks but the earthy combination of potato, asparagus and mushroom is particularly good.

Parsnip and Parmesan Loaf
served with a Fennel and Olive Medley
Serves 6

Loaf:

450g	Parsnips
2	Leeks – cut lengthways
4	Eggs
1^1/$_4$ cups (120g)	Parmesan
^{1}/$_2$ bunch	Thyme – leaves only
^{1}/$_3$ cup (80mL)	Cream
	Salt and pepper

Fennel and Olive Medley:

3 bulbs	Fennel (young)
6 cloves	Garlic – cut in half
6	Eschalots – peeled and cut in half
18	Kalamata olives
1^1/$_3$ cup (80 mL)	Olive oil
1 tbls	Balsamic vinegar
^{1}/$_3$ cup (80mL)	Vegetable stock
4	Roasted tomatoes (See Basics, p147)
	Loaf tin (25 x 10cm) – brushed with butter and some of the grated Parmesan (extra)

Preheat the oven to 170°C.

Boil the parsnips till they have softened enough to slice into lengths with ease. Blanch the leeks in boiling water for about 45 seconds, and then refresh under cold water.

In a bowl, beat the eggs with the cream and parmesan and season with salt and pepper.

To assemble:
Lay parsnips on the bottom of the loaf tin, sprinkle with chopped thyme and pour on some of the egg mix. Continue to build up layers in this fashion, finishing with a top layer of parsnip.

Bake on the middle oven shelf for 45 minutes.

Allow to cool for 10 minutes before turning out.

For the medley:
Trim the outside of the fennel and cut into quarters.

In a heavy-based saucepan, heat the olive oil and sweat off the eschalots and garlic for a few minutes.

Add the fennel and toss around gently. Then add the olives, balsamic vinegar and vegetable stock. Reduce the heat to a very low simmer, cover with a lid and cook for 10–12 minutes, or until the fennel is tender.

Season well and, just before serving, add the roasted tomatoes and warm through. Sprinkle with shaved or grated parmesan.

Vegetable Torte
with Pumpkin and Couscous Pastry
Serves 6

For the casserole:

Choose whatever vegetables you have on hand; onions, garlic, ginger, celery, zucchini, eggplant, capsicum, spinach, mushrooms, etc.

1x425g tin	Tomatoes
1 quantity	Béchamel (see Basics, page 146)
1 tbls	Thyme
1 tbls	Rosemary
1 tsp	Ground coriander
$^1/_2$ tsp	Ground cumin
$^1/_4$ tsp	Cinnamon
2 tbls	Ketjap manis (Indonesian sweet soy)
	Salt and pepper
$^3/_4$ cup (100g)	Cheddar
	Olive oil

Pumpkin and Couscous Pastry:

600g	Pumpkin – peeled
$2^1/_4$ cup (400g)	Couscous
1 cup (80g)	Breadcrumbs (fresh preferable)
1	Egg – beaten lightly
$^3/_4$ cup (100g)	Cheddar
2 tbls	Olive oil

In a heavy-based saucepan, sweat the onion, garlic and ginger in a little olive oil with the fresh herbs and spices.

Add the celery, zucchini, eggplant or capsicum (diced) and sweat for a further 5 minutes before adding the tomatoes (or homemade tomato sauce if you have it).

Reduce the heat and simmer for 40 minutes. The tomato should be well reduced by now, and the vegetables soft and tender. If there is still a lot of excess tomato juice, ladle it off and reserve it to use as a sauce. If you are using spinach or mushrooms, add these now and cook for a further few minutes before adding the béchamel sauce. Adjust the seasoning, adding the ketjap manis and salt and pepper and fold through the grated cheese. Remove from the heat and leave to cool.

To prepare the Pumpkin and Couscous Pastry:
Boil or steam the pumpkin. Drain and mash well.

Soften the couscous in boiled water for 10 minutes, then drain and add to the pumpkin.

Add the breadcrumbs, cheese, olive oil and egg and mix thoroughly.

Brush a 23cm springform tin lightly with oil. Preheat the oven to 180°C.

With your fingers, press in the pastry, making sure that it is evenly distributed over the bottom and sides to a thickness of about 1.5cm, a little thicker around the bottom rim of the tin.

To assemble:
Pour the vegetable mixture into the prepared tin and cover with the remaining pastry.

Place the springform tin on a flat baking tray and bake on the middle oven shelf for 45 – 60 minutes. The pastry should be golden and crisp.

It is best to rest the torte for at least 30 minutes before serving.

Serve with a crisp green salad, some roasted vegetables and olives.

The Secret
The tomato and vegetable casserole needs to be moist, but not swimming in liquid—skim off any excess liquid before adding the béchamel.

Pumpkin and couscous pastry will hold most fillings, provided they are not too runny. This particular torte stores well in the fridge.

rice

pasta, noodles and polenta

* Mushroom and Pea Risotta Cakes with Lemon and Thyme Sauce

* Scallop and Pumpkin Lasagne with Burnt Butter Sauce

* Grilled Polenta and Roasted Jerusalem Artichokes with Salad of Blue Cheese, Walnuts and Pears

* Baked Potato Gnocchi with Asparagus and Thyme

* Farfalle with Mushrooms, English Spinach, Hazelnuts and Parmesan

* Stuart's Ten Minute Raw Tomato Sauce

* Linguine with Grilled Tuna, Roasted Capsicum, Capers and Anchovies

* Ham Noodle Bake

* Pad Thai Noodles

* Frypan Polenta Bread with Mushrooms

* Golden Nugget Pumpkin with BBQ Pork, Hokkien Noodles and Coconut

* Chicken Liver and Rosemary Risotto with Deep-fried Cabbage

* Indian Lamb and Rice Torte

Mushroom and Pea Risotto Cakes
with Lemon and Thyme Sauce
Serves 6

30g	Dried porcini mushrooms
2 cups (500mL)	Vegetable stock
2 cups (440g)	Arborio rice
1 cup (155g)	Green peas – boiled
$^3/_4$ cup (115g)	Parmesan – grated
1	Onion (large) – chopped
2 cloves	Garlic – minced
3 tbls	Olive oil
1 tbls	Thyme
	Plain flour
	Salt and pepper
	Vegetable oil
	Lemon and Thyme Sauce:
5 tbls (100mL)	White wine
$1^1/_4$ cup (300mL)	Cream
2 tbls	Thyme leaves (lemon scented)
100g	Unsalted butter – cut into pieces
	Juice of $1^1/_2$ lemons
	Salt and pepper

Cover the porcini mushrooms in warm water and leave them to soak for $^1/_2$ hour. Squeeze all the water from the mushrooms and pour the porcini water through a very fine sieve. Add this porcini water to the vegetable stock and bring the liquid to a slow simmer. Chop the mushrooms and set to one side.

In a heavy-based saucepan heat the oil and add the garlic and onion. Cook just a couple of minutes before adding the rice. Cook this mixture till the rice is translucent.

Gradually begin to incorporate the warm stock, cooking and stirring constantly until all the stock has been absorbed. The rice should almost be cooked. Now add the peas, chopped porcini, thyme, and parmesan. Mix well and season with salt and pepper.

Allow the risotto to cool for at least 1/2 hour.

Shape the risotto into flat patties and pass gently through the flour to coat. Shallow-fry the risotto cakes in hot oil in a large frying pan. Drain on absorbent paper and serve warm with the Lemon and Thyme Sauce.

To prepare the sauce:
Bring the wine to the boil and reduce by two thirds.

Add the cream and thyme. Gently simmer till cream has slightly thickened.

Remove from direct heat and whisk in the butter.

Finish with the lemon juice, salt and pepper.

The risotto can be made a day in advance and refrigerated, this will certainly make it easier when it comes to shaping the cakes. Also, transformed with the help of this simple sauce, these cakes are a great way to use up leftover risotto.

SCALLOP AND PUMPKIN LASAGNE
WITH BURNT BUTTER SAUCE
SERVES 6

12	Square lasagne sheets
1kg	Pumpkin – cooked, mashed and kept warm
18	Sage leaves
36	Scallops
250g	Butter
$^1/_2$ cup (125g)	Mustard Fruits – chopped (see Basics, page 145)
1 tbls	Olive oil
2 tbls	Almonds – chopped (skin on)
	Salt and pepper

Heat the olive oil in a frying pan and cook the scallops for 2 minutes only. Season well with salt and pepper and set to one side, keeping them warm.

Cook the lasagne sheets in boiling salted water and drain. Place a lasagne sheet on the bottom of each serving plate. Spoon on a layer of mashed pumpkin and mustard fruits, then the scallops. Season well with salt and pepper and finish with another sheet of lasagne.

Melt the butter in a saucepan till it turns a light brown colour and throw in the sage leaves and the chopped almonds. Spoon this mixture over each lasagne and serve immediately.

Making a great light meal or entrée, this dish works equally well with scallops or prawns. Mustard fruits are very easy to prepare, bringing with them a rich and exotic flavour but if time does not allow and you can't get hold of them at the deli, it's delicious enough without them.

rice, pasta, noodles & polenta

99

GRILLED POLENTA AND ROASTED JERUSALEM ARTICHOKES
WITH A SALAD OF BLUE CHEESE, WALNUTS AND PEARS

SERVES 6

1 quantity	Polenta (see Basics, page 146)
18	Jerusalem artichokes
1 whole head	Garlic – broken into cloves (unpeeled)
150g	A soft creamy blue cheese, such as a delicate King Island Blue
3	Pears
1 bunch	Rocket, or mixed salad leaves
2 sprigs	Fresh thyme leaves only
24	Walnut halves
	Balsamic vinegar
	Olive oil
	Salt and pepper

Prepare the polenta and pour onto a flat baking tray. Allow it to cool completely.

Preheat the oven to 220°C.

Cut the Jerusalem artichokes in half and place them in a roasting tin with the garlic cloves and thyme leaves. Season well with salt and pepper and spoon over enough olive oil to coat the artichokes well enough for roasting. Roast the artichokes till they are nice and soft.

Slice the blue cheese and set to one side.

Peel the pears and cut into eighths.

Pick over the rocket and discard any tough stalks. Break the leaves into a big bowl and add the walnuts, sliced pears, and the blue cheese. Toss the salad gently with olive oil, balsamic vinegar, salt and pepper to taste.

To grill the polenta, cut the firm polenta into wedges and brush both sides very well with olive oil. Grill for a couple of minutes on each side so that both sides become crisp and golden.

To assemble salad:
Place the warm polenta on each plate. Then the rocket, blue cheese salad and finish with the roasted garlic and Jerusalem artichokes.

Shavings of parmesan can be added as a garnish if desired.

Perfect as a light lunch or entrée, this gorgeous combination of lingering flavours will take you by surprise.

BAKED POTATO GNOCCHI
WITH ASPARAGUS AND THYME
SERVES 6

1kg	Potatoes – peeled
2 cloves	Garlic – peeled
$^3/_4$ cup (100g)	Plain flour
150g	Ricotta
4	Egg yolks
1/2 bunch	Fresh thyme
	Pinch of nutmeg
2 bunches	Asparagus – trimmed of rough stalky ends
$1^1/_2$ cups (150g)	Parmesan – freshly grated
$1^1/_4$ cup (300mL)	Cream
5 tbls (100mL)	Milk
150g	Gippsland Blue cheese
5 tbs (100mL)	White wine
	Olive oil
	Salt and pepper

Bring the potatoes and garlic to the boil in salted water. When soft, mash till free of lumps. Fold in the sifted flour, ricotta, egg yolks, and parmesan, mixing thoroughly. Season well with salt, pepper, and nutmeg. Pour the mixture onto a well oiled baking tray. Cover in plastic wrap and set to cool in the refrigerator for at least 2 hours.

Preheat the oven to 200°C.

Cut the potato gnocchi into 6 squares, place on a baking tray, brush well with olive oil and bake for 15 minutes.

Whilst the gnocchi is baking, place the wine in a heavy-based saucepan and reduce by one third. Adding the cream and milk, simmer gently till slightly thickened. Gradually whisk in the blue cheese and thyme leaves.

Blanch the asparagus in boiling salted water.

To serve:
Place the gnocchi onto each plate, scatter the asparagus over and top with the blue cheese sauce. Serve with extra parmesan, if desired, and a fresh green salad.

Variations:
Alternatives to serve with the gnocchi could be:

* Roasted garlic, walnuts, parmesan and basil.

* Ricotta, prosciutto and wilted spinach.

* Roasted Tomatoes, black olives and Pesto (see Basics, pages 147 and 151).

* Shredded chicken, fennel and leek, with mascarpone.

* Zucchini, sage, pecorino and pine nuts.

Gnocchi can be made in advance and kept in the fridge till needed. If you're not particularly fond of blue cheese, other cheeses can be substituted.

Farfalle with Mushrooms,
English Spinach, Hazelnuts and Parmesan
Serves 6

750g	Farfalle pasta
60g	Dried mushrooms
	(such as porcini or shiitake)
200g	Fresh field mushrooms
1 bunch (500g)	English spinach
1 cup (150g)	Hazelnuts – toasted, skinned and
	chopped
2 cloves	Garlic – minced
75g	Butter
4 tbls	Olive oil
200ml	Cream
18	Sage leaves – roughly chopped
	Pinch of nutmeg
	Parmesan
	Salt and pepper

To make the mushroom sauce:
Soak the dried mushrooms in boiling water to cover for 25 minutes. Strain the dried mushrooms and keep the liquid to one side. Chop the mushrooms. Slice the field mushrooms thinly.

In a saucepan, melt the butter and 2 tablespoons of the olive oil together, add the garlic and sage and then add the two types of mushrooms. Sauté for about 5 minutes before adding the cream and some of the reserved mushroom water. Season well with salt and pepper and the nutmeg. Reduce this sauce for a further 4 minutes.

Pick over the spinach leaves, discarding the long stems, and wash thoroughly. In a wok or frying pan, heat 1 tablespoon of oil till hot. Throw in the spinach and cook briskly, until the leaves have just begun to wilt. Remove from the wok and set to one side.

To cook the pasta:
Place hazelnuts on a flat baking tray in the oven (180°C). Roast till brown and remove. When cool enough to be handled, rub through fingers to remove skin. It's not necessary to remove every last little bit of skin.

Bring a large pot of water to the boil with salt and the remaining 1 tablespoon of olive oil. Drop in the farfalle and stir with a wooden spoon till the water has returned to the boil. Cook till 'al dente'. Drain the pasta well and add it to the mushroom sauce, mixing well so that the sauce cooks the pasta. Fold through the wilted spinach and hazelnuts. Serve immediately with shaved parmesan cheese.

The roasted hazelnuts and dried mushrooms work beautifully together.

STUART'S TEN MINUTE
RAW TOMATO SAUCE
SERVES 6–8

1 kg	Ripe, fresh, juicy tomatoes
2 cloves	Garlic – chopped finely
2	Green shallots – chopped
20 leaves	Basil
	Olive oil (a flavoursome extra virgin)
500g	Pasta of your choice (fresh is best)
	Parmesan – shaved
	Salt and pepper

Wash the tomatoes thoroughly.

Cut in half and remove the seeds over a sieve.

Cut the tomato cheeks into squares and place in a large bowl.

Press the juice from the seeds over the tomato flesh.

Add the green shallots, garlic and basil to the tomatoes and season well with salt and pepper.

Cover in olive oil and, if possible, leave to marinate for at least 1 hour (the longer the better, even overnight however, if time is of the essence, this is perfectly delicious eaten straight away).

Boil the pasta of your choice and toss through the tomatoes (at room temperature).

Serve with shaved parmesan, green salad and wood-fired bread.

The extraordinary simplicity of this dish belies its abundance of sensual complexity. It's tempting to adventure on with the addition of, say, black or green olives or capers, anchovies, parsley, chives ... but there are few things more potent than a perfectly ripe summer tomato raised to poetic heights by such simple means.

LINGUINE
WITH GRILLED TUNA,
ROASTED CAPSICUM, CAPERS
AND ANCHOVIES
SERVES 4–6

2	Red capsicum – roasted, skinned, seeded and sliced
1	Yellow capsicum – roasted, skinned, seeded and sliced (see Basics, page 147)
2 large	Ripe tomatoes – peeled, seeded, and chopped
1 tbls	Capers – chopped
1 tbls	Caper juice
2 cloves	Garlic – peeled and chopped
6	Anchovy fillets (according to taste)
12	Basil leaves – chopped roughly
2 tbls	Parsley – chopped
4 tbls	Olive oil
	Salt and pepper
400g	Linguine
600g	Tuna – cut into 3 pieces

In a large bowl, combine the capsicums, tomatoes, capers, caper juice, garlic, anchovies, basil, parsley and olive oil. Season with salt and pepper. Set to one side.

Bring a large pot of boiling salted water to the boil and cook the linguine. While the linguine is cooking, heat a grill plate or heavy-based frying pan with a little extra olive oil. When very hot, quickly sear the tuna on both sides. Dice the cooked tuna, add to the tomatoes and capsicums and toss this mixture through the warm cooked pasta.

Ham Noodle Bake

Serves 6–8

100g	Butter
1	Onion (large) – chopped
2 sticks	Celery – chopped
2 cloves	Garlic – minced
100g	Plain flour
4 cups (1 Litre)	Milk
200g	Leg ham – chopped
1 cup (100g)	Parmesan
$^3/_4$ cup (100g)	Cheddar
$^1/_2$ bunch	Parsley – chopped
2	Egg yolks – beaten
	Pinch of nutmeg
	Salt and pepper
500g	Penne – cooked (hot)

Preheat the oven to 180°C

Melt the butter in a heavy-based saucepan, add the onion, celery and garlic and cook for a couple of minutes.

Stir in the flour and cook further for a few minutes.

Slowly add the milk, a little at a time, making sure you beat well to avoid lumps.

Once all the milk has been incorporated, reduce the heat and let the sauce simmer for 10 minutes, stirring occasionally.

Add the ham, cheeses, and parsley to the sauce, mixing through well before adding the egg yolks. Season well with nutmeg, salt and pepper. Remove from the heat immediately, pour the sauce onto the pasta and mix the sauce through completely.

Brush a 23cm springform tin with olive oil and pour in the pasta mix.

Place the tin on a flat baking tray and bake for 1 hour.

This dish is best left to rest for an hour, at least, before cutting. Serve warm or at room temperature.

An ideal dish to make the day before. Serves well with a crisp green salad, Roasted Tomatoes (see Basics, page 147) and basil.

rice, pasta, noodles & polenta

105

PAD THAI NOODLES

SERVES 6

3 tbls	Sugar
$^1/_3$ cup (80mL)	Tamarind water
	(see Glossary, page 155)
$^1/_4$ cup (60mL)	Thai fish sauce
2 tbls	Rice vinegar
2 tsp	Paprika
2 tbls	Vegetable oil
4 cloves	Garlic – chopped finely
1	Dried red chilli – chopped finely
1 cup (185g)	Firm tofu – diced
1	Telegraph cucumber – diced
250g packet	Rice noodles – soaked in cold water
	until soft, then drained
2 cups (180g)	Bean sprouts
1 bunch	Garlic chives – chopped roughly
$^1/_2$ cup (80g)	Peanuts – ground and toasted
	Salt and pepper
	Coriander leaves – for garnish
	Fresh lime – cut in quarters for garnish

In a small bowl combine the sugar, tamarind water, fish sauce, vinegar and paprika and set to one side.

Heat the oil in a large wok and stir-fry the garlic and chilli. Add the tofu and cucumber and stir-fry for 1 minute.

Add the fish sauce mixture to the wok and then stir-fry in the noodles, bean sprouts, and garlic chives.

Finally, add the ground peanuts, salt and pepper to taste.

Serve garnished with the coriander and fresh lime.

You can add chicken or prawns, if desired.

Simply put pad thai noodles are stir-fry noodles, 'Thai-style'. Its unique signature is in the combining of the sugar, vinegar and chilli during cooking, coating the noodles in a deeply satisfying mixture of tastes.

FRYING PAN POLENTA BREAD
WITH MUSHROOMS
SERVES 4

FOR THE BREAD:

$^1/_2$ cup (75g)	Polenta
$^1/_2$ cup (75g)	Plain flour
2 tsp	Baking powder
1/4 tsp	Salt
1	Egg
$^3/_4$ cup (185mL)	Milk
$1^1/_2$ tbls	Olive oil

MUSHROOMS:

1	Leek – sliced finely and washed well
1 clove	Garlic – minced
2 tbls	Olive oil
500g	Mixed mushrooms (fresh) – sliced
8	Sage leaves
5 tbls (100mL)	Stock (chicken or vegetable)
150mL	Cream
	Pinch of nutmeg
	Salt and pepper

Preheat the oven to 220ºC. Place a heavy-based ovenproof frying pan in the oven to get very hot.

Mix the polenta, flour, baking powder and salt in a bowl.

Combine the egg, milk and olive oil and slowly add this to the dry ingredients mixing until smooth.

Remove the frying pan from the oven and brush with extra olive oil.

Pour in the polenta mixture and place back in the oven for 10 minutes.

To prepare the mushrooms:
In a frying pan, sauté the leek and garlic in the olive oil.

Now add the mushrooms and sage leaves.

After a few minutes add the stock and reduce for a few minutes before adding the cream.

Allow this mixture to simmer gently for a few more minutes. Season well with nutmeg, salt and pepper.

Remove the bread from the oven and pour on the mushrooms.

Return to the oven for 10 minutes. Serve hot from the frying pan with a crisp green salad.

Variations:
Replace the mushrooms with:

* Ratatouille (see recipe for Peppered Minute Steak with Ratatouille and Poached Egg, page 115)

* Bolognaise sauce

* Creamed spinach with ricotta and parmesan

* Rich tomato sauce with crab, chilli and prawns

* Sautéed cabbage, bacon, onion and sage, in a cheese sauce

The Secret
Have the frying pan extremely hot before pouring in the polenta mix. This will help seal the bottom to a crisp and crunchy finish.

GOLDEN NUGGET PUMPKINS
WITH BBQ PORK, HOKKIEN NOODLES AND COCONUT

SERVES 6

6	Golden nugget pumpkins
	Vegetable oil
	Sesame oil
2 cloves	Garlic – minced
$^1/_2$	Red capsicum – sliced
$^1/_2$	Green capsicum – sliced
$^1/_2$ bunch	Green shallots – chopped
$1^3/_4$ cup (150g)	Fresh bean sprouts – washed and drained
1 bunch	Bok choy – washed and chopped roughly
600g	BBQ pork fillet – sliced
4 tbls	Ketjap manis (Indonesian sweet soy)
2 tbls	Fish sauce
$^3/_4$ cup	Coconut milk
	Juice of 1 lime
750g	Hokkien noodles
$^1/_2$ cup (80g)	Cashew nuts
$^1/_2$ bunch	Fresh coriander – chopped

Preheat the oven to 200°C.

Cut off the tops of the pumpkins and scoop out the seeds, place on a baking tray and drizzle over a little vegetable oil and sesame oil. Bake till the outside skin is almost blistered and the flesh is soft enough to eat.

In a large wok, heat 1 tablespoon vegetable oil and a drop more of sesame oil. When really hot, throw in the garlic, capsicum, onions, bean sprouts and bok choy and stir-fry quickly. Add the pork with the ketjap manis, fish sauce, coconut milk, and lime juice.

Pour some boiling water over the noodles, leave to stand for two minutes before draining and adding to the vegetables and pork. Finish with the cashews and freshly chopped coriander.

To serve, place a pumpkin in the middle of each serving plate and spoon in the noodles and some extra sauce.

Hokkien noodles and BBQ pork are available from Chinese supermarkets and food outlets. You can just as easily serve these noodles without the pumpkins, however they do bring a distinct flavouring and visually transform the meal.

Chicken Liver and Rosemary Risotto
with Deep-fried Cabbage
Serves 6

150g	Chicken livers – chopped in half
4 tbls	Olive oil
$^1/_2$ cup (125mL)	Vermouth
2 cups (500mL)	Chicken stock- warm
1	Onion – chopped finely
2 cloves	Garlic
1 cup (220g)	Arborio rice
1 sprig	Rosemary – chopped finely
$^1/_2$ cup (50g)	Parmesan
	Oil for deep-frying the cabbage
$^1/_4$	Savoy cabbage – shredded finely

Using a large, heavy-based frying pan, sauté the chicken livers in 2 tablespoons of hot olive oil for 2 minutes. Remove from the pan and set to one side.

Return the frying pan to the heat and swirl the vermouth around thoroughly, collecting all that remains from the livers. Add this to the chicken stock.

Sauté the onion and garlic in the remaining olive oil in a large heavy-based saucepan for a couple of minutes before adding the rice.

When the rice is translucent, add the rosemary and gradually begin to incorporate the warm chicken stock, cooking and stirring continually. Continue adding the chicken stock till it has all been absorbed and the rice is cooked.

Now add the chicken livers and mix through well. Finally, mix in the parmesan.

To prepare the cabbage:
Heat the oil in a deep saucepan. Fry the cabbage till golden brown. Drain on absorbent paper and sprinkle with salt. Serve as a garnish for the chicken liver risotto.

For lovers of chicken liver, this is a real treat. If you can't be bothered deep-frying the cabbage, just lightly stir-fry it with a little olive oil.

INDIAN LAMB
AND RICE TORTE
SERVES 8

1 kg	Diced lamb shoulder
2	Onions – diced
2cm piece	Ginger – grated
6	Cardamom pods
4 cloves	Garlic – minced
1 $^1/_2$ tsp	Garam masala
1 tbls	Tomato purée
$^3/_4$ cup (200mL)	Coconut milk
1 bunch	Coriander – chopped
2	Tomatoes – chopped
1 or 2	Fresh green chillies – chopped finely
1 tsp	Cumin
3 cups	Basmati rice – cooked
1 tub (200g)	Plain yoghurt
2	Egg yolks
100g	Butter or ghee – melted
6	Curry leaves
3 tbls	Vegetable oil

Preheat the oven to 220°C.

To make lamb curry:
Place the vegetable oil in a heavy, flameproof casserole and, when hot, add the onions, ginger, green chillies, cardamom pods, curry leaves, garlic, ground cumin and garam masala. Stir over a high heat for 2 minutes, before adding the tomato purée and a little water to moisten.

Place the lamb on a flat baking tray and roast for 10–15 minutes or till the meat has browned. Place the lamb in the casserole, cover and cook gently, stirring frequently, for 1 hour.

Add the coconut milk and cook for a further 10 minutes. Remove from heat and stir in the fresh coriander. Reduce the oven temperature to 180°C.

To assemble:
In a large bowl, combine the cooked rice, yoghurt and egg yolks with half the melted butter or ghee. With the remaining ghee, thoroughly brush the sides of a 24cm springform tin. Press some of the rice mixture into the base and around the sides of the tin, making sure that there are no gaps and that it is evenly distributed. Pour in the lamb and cover with the remaining rice. Cover with foil and bake 1 $^1/_2$ hours. The rice should be golden and crispy.

To serve:
Remove from the oven and allow to cool for at least 15 minutes before unmoulding.

Serve with a salad made from the fresh tomatoes, green shallots and coriander.

The Secret
Don't be shy about the amount of butter used to coat the tin. The desired result is a crisp, golden crust that glistens with butter and meat juices.

meat
and fish

* Poached Shoulder of Lamb with Herb and Anchovy Dressing

* Peppered Minute Steak served with Ratatouille and Poached Egg

* Grilled Salmon with Chickpea Salad

* Soy Poached Deep Sea Perch with Ginger Mayonnaise

* Warm Salad of Corned Beef with a Compote of Potato, Mustard, Leeks and Celery

* Grilled Tuna with Mick's Green Rice and Spicy Tomato Salsa

* Indian Chicken and Eggplant Cutlets with a Roasted Pumpkin Salad
  and Yogurt and Cashew Sauce

* Chicken B'stilla Served with Watercress, Orange and Olive Salad

* BBQ Duck Cakes with Ginger, Lime and Pawpaw Salsa

* Gumbo Ya Ya

* Robyn's Braised Lamb Shanks with Lemon, Olives, and Basil

* BBQ Lamb Kofta and Couscous and Apricot Salad and a Tahini and Yogurt Dressing

POACHED SHOULDER OF LAMB
WITH HERB AND ANCHOVY DRESSING

2$^1/_2$ kg	Shoulder of lamb – rolled and tied (your butcher will do this for you)
	Chicken stock to cover lamb
1	Onion – cut in quarters
1	Carrot – chopped roughly
2 sticks	Celery – chopped roughly
1 whole head	Garlic – cut in half
2 sprigs	Thyme
2 sprigs	Sage
2 sprigs	Rosemary
3	Bay leaves
100mL	White wine

HERB AND ANCHOVY DRESSING

2	Egg yolks
1 heaped tsp	Dijon mustard
1 tbls	Wine vinegar
2 cloves	Garlic
1 heaped tsp	Capers
3–4	Anchovy fillets (to taste)
10	Basil leaves
$^1/_2$ bunch	Flat-leaf parsley – leaves only
150mL	Olive oil
2 tbls	Warm water
	Salt and pepper

Using a heavy-based frying pan, and a little hot oil, brown the lamb all over and then place it in a stockpot. Add the stock, wine, vegetables and herbs.

Bring to a rapid boil and reduce to simmer for 1$^1/_2$ hours, being careful not to cook to quickly as this will toughen the meat.

When cooked, place 2 cups of the lamb stock in a small saucepan and reduce to use as a glaze.

To prepare the Herb and Anchovy Dressing:
Place the egg yolks, mustard and vinegar in food processor and blend together.

Add the garlic, capers and anchovies and process further. Slowly drizzle in the olive oil with the processor still running. If the dressing becomes too thick, thin it down with the water and a little caper liquid.

Now add herbs and process until fully incorporated, adding a little of the lamb stock if you prefer it a little runnier. Season well with salt and pepper.

Dress the lamb with the dressing and some of the reduced stock and serve with some fresh salad greens, tomatoes and green beans.

Don't make the mistake of thinking that poaching is difficult. The results of this simple meal—tender, juicy and fragrant—will speak for themselves.

PEPPERED MINUTE STEAK
WITH RATATOUILLE AND POACHED EGG

SERVES 6

6	Minute steaks
6	Free-range eggs – poached
	RATATOUILLE:
2	Eggplants – cut into 3cm cubes
2	Onions – chopped
3 cloves	Garlic – minced
3	Zucchini – cut into 3cm cubes
2	Red capsicums – seeded and cut into 3cm cubes
1	Green capsicum – seeded and cut into 3cm cubes
5	Ripe tomatoes – peeled, seeded, and chopped
1 tbls	Fresh thyme – chopped
	Basil leaves – chopped
	Parsley – chopped
100mL	Olive oil
	Salt and pepper

For the Ratatouille:
Place the eggplant in a colander, sprinkle with salt and pepper and leave for 30 minutes. Rinse well and pat dry with absorbent paper.

Place the oil in a large, heavy-based flameproof casserole and sauté the onions, garlic and thyme for a couple of minutes before adding the zucchini, capsicum, eggplant, and tomatoes.

Season well with salt and pepper and cover casserole with a lid. Reduce heat to a low simmer and cook for one hour, stirring mixture occasionally.

Add the fresh basil leaves just before serving.

For the steaks:
Heat a little extra oil in the base of a heavy-based frying pan. Grind some fresh black pepper onto each side of the steaks. When oil is really hot, add the steaks and sear briefly on each side, about 1 minute. Meanwhile, poach the eggs.

To serve:
Place the ratatouille on the base of each plate and place the steak on the top. Finish with a poached egg and garnish with chopped parsley.

The Secret
Don't over cook the eggs. The yolk should be runny enough so that, when cut, it blends and becomes a part of the sauce. Delicious.

Grilled Salmon
with Chickpea Salad
Serves 6

6	Salmon cutlets

For Chickpeas:

$^3/_4$ cup (165g)	Dried chickpeas – soaked for at least 2 hours in cold water
1	Onion – cut in half
2	Carrots – chopped roughly
1 stick	Celery – chopped roughly
2 cloves	Garlic – crushed
2 sprigs	Fresh thyme
3-4	Bay leaves
2 tbls	Olive oil

Drain the chickpeas and place in a saucepan with all the other ingredients. Cover with cold water, bring to the boil and cook for about 50 minutes or until the chickpeas are tender. Keep in liquid till ready to use. (If you prefer not to cook your own chickpeas, omit this step and substitute with pre-cooked, canned or vacuum-packed chickpeas.)

For the Salad:

1 bunch	English spinach – picked and washed well
1	Onion (large) – chopped finely
2	Carrots – chopped fairly small
1 stick	Celery – chopped fairly small
4	Tomatoes – blanched, peeled, seeded and chopped roughly
1 clove	Garlic – minced
12 leaves	Basil – chopped
$^1/_2$ bunch	Flat-leaf parsley – chopped
250mL	Dry white wine
	Extra virgin olive oil – to coat the spinach
	Juice of 2 lemons

In a heavy-based saucepan, heat a little olive oil and sweat off the garlic, onion, carrots and celery till tender.

Add the white wine and reduce until almost fully evaporated.

Add the chopped tomato, spinach and drained chickpeas. Cook for a further few minutes, seasoning well.

Remove from heat and add the olive oil, lemon juice, basil and parsley. Serve warm with the grilled salmon and lemon wedges.

To grill the salmon: Brush each of the steaks with olive oil and place onto a very hot grill plate. Cook for 2 minutes on each side and serve straight away. The salmon should remain a little pink on the inside.

Variations:
This chickpea salad lends itself well to grilled chicken thighs as well as most varieties of grilled fish.

Soy Poached Deep Sea Pearch
with Ginger Mayonnaise
Serves 4

4 x 100g fillets	Deep sea perch
2 cups (500mL)	Water
2cm piece	Ginger – cut into rounds
2 tbls	Light soy sauce
1 tbls	Butter
1 bunch	Baby bok choy –
	washed and trimmed
4 serves	Brown rice
6–8 tbls	Mayonnaise
	(see Basics, page 150), mixed with
	$^1/_2$ tblsp Fresh ginger

In a large frying pan, bring the water to the boil with the soy sauce and rounds of ginger. Reduce for a couple of minutes before gently placing the deep sea perch, skin side up, into the stock.

Lower the heat and poach gently for 2 minutes before turning the fillets over for a further 2 minutes.

Gently remove the fillets and keep them warm on a plate covered with foil.

Reduce the stock further before adding the trimmed bok choy, the butter, and cooking until soft and tender, about 2 minutes.

Serve on a bed of warm brown rice with the bok choy, and some of the poaching liquid spooned over the fish. Ginger mayonnaise is the perfect accompaniment.

I know brown rice gets a lot of bad press. It is in this case, however, the ideal choice with its nuttiness and texture the perfect match for the firmness of the fish. I prefer to pressure cook rice which not only reduces the cooking time to around 15 minutes but greatly enhances its redeeming qualities.

Warm Salad of Corned Beef
with Compote of Potatoes, Mustard, Leeks and Celery

Serves 6

For the beef:

1$^{1}/_{2}$ kg piece	Corned beef (silverside)
1	Onion – cut in half
2	Carrots – peeled and cut in four
3 sticks	Celery – cut in four
2	Bay leaves
2 sprigs	Thyme
2	Cloves
6	Peppercorns

Compote ingredients:

10	Chat potatoes – boiled and cut in half
12	Baby leeks (if unavailable, 6 thin leeks)
4 sticks	Celery
1 bunch	Watercress – picked over and washed well
100mL	Olive oil (good quality)
50mL	Red wine vinegar
1 tsp	Black mustard seeds
1 $^{1}/_{2}$ tbls	Dijon mustard
	Salt and pepper
	Horseradish – for serving

Place the silverside in a large stockpot, cover with cold water and add the celery, carrots, onion, bay leaves, thyme, cloves and peppercorns.

Bring to the boil, then reduce the heat and cook for 2 hours, skimming the surface of any residue throughout. You may need to keep topping up the water as you go.

For the Compote:
Slice the leeks lengthways and wash thoroughly. Cut into 5 – 6cm lengths.

Cut the celery into four lengthways and then into 5 – 6cm lengths.

Blanch the celery and leeks in boiling water for 5 minutes and then refresh thoroughly under cold water.

In a bowl, combine the celery and leeks with the potatoes and watercress and set to one side till needed. (This salad should be served at room temperature, so if you don't intend to use it immediately, wait before adding the watercress).

In a small bowl, combine the mustard, mustard seeds, vinegar and olive oil. Just before serving, add 2 tablespoons of the warm beef poaching liquid. Season well with salt and pepper and add to the compote.

To serve:
Slice the corned beef very thinly and toss it through the compote of vegetables.

Serve with extra mustard and horseradish.

GRILLED TUNA
WITH MICK'S GREEN RICE AND SPICY TOMATO SALSA
SERVES 6

6	Tuna steaks about 150g each – skin removed
	GREEN RICE:
2 cups	Long grain rice
6	Spring onions (with green tops) – chopped finely
1 bunch (500g)	English spinach – washed, blanched and finely chopped
1 bunch	Watercress – picked from coarse stalks, washed and chopped finely
1/2 bunch	Coriander (stalks included) – chopped finely
1 bunch (500g)	Flat-leaf parsley – chopped finely
3 cloves	Garlic – minced
1 – 2	Green chillies – seeds removed and chopped finely
2 cups (500mL)	Chicken stock
2 tbls	Olive oil
40g	Butter
	Salt and pepper
1 quantity	Mick's Spicy Tomato Salsa (See Basics, page 149)

To cook the rice:
Heat the oil and the butter in a heavy bottomed saucepan.

Add the rice and stir for 1 minute before adding the spring onions, spinach, watercress, coriander, parsley, garlic and chilli.

Cook for 1 minute before adding the warm chicken stock, salt and pepper.

Bring to the boil and then reduce heat to a very slow simmer. Cover with a lid and leave it to cook for 20 minutes.

To serve:
Lightly brush each of the tuna steaks with olive oil and sear on a very hot grill or BBQ for about 1 minute on each side. More if you prefer well done.

Serve the tuna on a bed of green rice and spoon over some tomato salsa.

This is an easy dish to prepare in advance. Just re-warm the rice and grill the tuna at the last moment.

meat and fish

121

Indian Chicken and Eggplant Cutlets
with Roasted Pumpkin Salad and Yoghurt and Cashew Sauce
Serves 6

Poached Chicken:

1.6 kg	Chicken
4 cloves	Garlic – cut in half
2 cm piece	Fresh ginger
3	Curry leaves
1	Cinnamon quill
4	Cardamom pods
	Peel of 1 lemon – cut into strips

For the Cutlets:

1	Eggplant – cut into 2cm dice
2	Onions – one cut in half and one into half-moon slices
2 sticks	Celery – chopped finely
2 tbls	Eggplant pickle (optional)
2	Eggs – beaten
2 tbls	Plain yoghurt
$^2/_3$ cup (100g)	Breadcrumbs
$^1/_3$ cup (60g)	Cashews – ground
$^1/_2$ bunch	Fresh coriander – chopped
	Chopped fresh red chilli – to taste
	Vegetable oil – for frying
3 cloves	Garlic – minced
2 cm piece	Fresh ginger – chopped finely
$^1/_2$ tsp	Fennel seeds
1 tsp	Ground cumin
1 tsp	Ground coriander
2 tsp	Garam masala
$^1/_2$ tsp	Ground turmeric

Crumbing ingredients:

Plain Flour

Egg whites (lightly beaten)

Breadcrumbs – for coating

To poach the chicken, place it in a stockpot with all the poaching ingredients. Cover in cold water and bring to the boil. Reduce the heat and gently poach for 1 hour or till cooked.

Cool the chicken in the liquid for another hour, then transfer it to a large plate.

When the chicken is cool enough to handle, remove all the flesh from the bones and chop the flesh finely, including a small amount of skin. Strain the stock and set to one side.

To prepare the cutlets, salt the eggplant, leaving it to drain in a colander for 1 hour. Rinse and pat dry.

Heat a little vegetable oil in a frying pan and cook the eggplant till soft and tender. It's probably best to do this in a couple of lots. Once cooked, remove from the pan and drain on absorbent paper to remove excess oil. Set to one side in a large bowl.

Heat a little more oil in the frying pan, add the fennel seeds and ground spices and cook till very aromatic. Add the onions, celery, garlic, and ginger and sauté till the onions are soft.

Add to the eggplant with the chopped chicken, the beaten eggs, yoghurt, breadcrumbs, ground almonds, eggplant pickle and fresh coriander. Season well with salt, pepper and chopped chilli to taste. Mix thoroughly and chill the mixture for 1 hour.

Take one handful of the mixture and gently shape it as close as possible into a cutlet shape (if this feels too fiddly, just shape into rissoles). Pass these cutlets through the flour, egg wash, and breadcrumbs to coat. Place on a flat tray and refrigerate till required.

To cook, heat some oil in a frying pan and gently cook the chicken cutlets till golden on each side. Serve with the pumpkin salad and yoghurt sauce.

ROASTED PUMPKIN
AND BLACK MUSTARD SEED SALAD
SERVES 4 – 6

1kg	Pumpkin – cut into cubes and roasted till soft
$^1/_2$	Red capsicum – cut into small dice
4	Green shallots – finely sliced
1 cm piece	Ginger – grated
1 tsp	Black mustard seed
1 tsp	Ground cumin
12	Mint leaves – finely shredded
	DRESSING
	Juice of 2 limes
$^1/_2$ tsp	Brown sugar
100mL	Coconut milk
1 tbls	Mango chutney

Mix all ingredients together while the pumpkin is still hot from the oven. Stir the dressing ingredients well and pour over the pumpkin.

YOGHURT
AND CASHEW SAUCE
SERVES 4 – 6

1 cup (250g)	Greek-style plain yoghurt
1 clove	Garlic – crushed
1 tbls	Chopped fresh coriander
1 tbls	Chopped fresh mint
$^1/_2$ tsp	Ground cumin
$^1/_4$ tsp	Ground turmeric
2 tbls	Lemon juice
$^1/_4$ cup (60g)	Cashews – toasted

To prepare the yoghurt sauce, grind the cashews with the cumin, turmeric, and garlic. Mix with the yoghurt and other ingredients. Chill until needed

I'll admit this recipe is quite time consuming to prepare but its well worth the extra effort. It looks—and tastes—great.

Chicken B'Stilla
(Moroccan chicken pie)

Serves 4–6

POACHED CHICKEN:

1.8 kg	Chicken
1	Onion – peeled
2 cm piece	Fresh ginger – halved
6 cloves	Garlic – peeled
1	Cinnamon quill
2 sprigs	Fresh coriander
	Rinds of $^1/_2$ lemon and $^1/_2$ orange (removed with a vegetable peeler)

OTHER INGREDIENTS:

1 tbls	Olive oil
2	Onions – chopped
4 cloves	Garlic – chopped finely
2 cm piece	Ginger – chopped finely
1 tbls	Ground turmeric
2 tsp	Ground coriander
2 tsp	Ground cumin
$1^1/_4$ tsp	Ground cinnamon
1 bunch	Fresh coriander (stalks and leaves) – chopped
$^1/_2$ bunch	Flat-leaf parsley – chopped
2	Eggs – beaten
$^1/_2$ cup (125g)	Coarsely chopped almonds
12 sheets	Filo pastry
1 tbls	Caster sugar
	Butter – for brushing
	Ground cinnamon – to taste

To poach the chicken, place it in a large saucepan with the poaching ingredients and cover with cold water. Bring to the boil, reduce the heat gently and poach for one hour, or until the chicken is tender. Remove the chicken from the stock and cool. Discard the skin, remove the flesh from the bone and shred. Strain the poaching stock and reduce 1 cup of the stock by half. (Keep remaining stock.)

Heat the oil in a saucepan and cook the onions over medium heat till soft and lightly coloured. Add the garlic, ginger and ground spices, cooking and stirring till aromatic.

Remove from the heat and stir in the shredded chicken and freshly chopped coriander and parsley. Moisten with a little of the reduced poaching stock and then stir in the eggs and almonds.

Preheat the oven to 180°C.

Combine the sugar and cinnamon. Layer the filo on your benchtop, brushing each sheet liberally with melted butter and then sprinkling lightly with the cinnamon sugar. Line the base of a buttered 5cm deep, 20 x 25cm baking dish with the filo, leaving the excess to overhang on one side.

Fill the dish with the chicken mixture and fold the overhanging filo over the top to cover. Brush the top with butter and sprinkle with a little more cinnamon sugar.

Bake for 25 minutes or until the pastry is golden.

Serve with a watercress, orange and olive salad.

WATERCRESS, ORANGE
AND OLIVE SALAD
SERVES 4

1 bunch	Watercress
2–3	Oranges
100g	Black Kalamata olives, pitted
1 clove	Garlic – finely chopped
100mL	Olive oil
	Juice of 1 lemon
1 tsp	Honey
	Salt and Pepper
	Toasted sesame seeds – for garnish

Remove skin from oranges and slice across-ways finely.

Pick over the watercress and refresh in cold water. Spin dry and place in bowl with the pitted olives and the orange slices.

Make dressing by placing finely chopped garlic, olive oil, lemon juice, salt, pepper, and tsp of honey in a jar and shaking well.

Pour over salad and sprinkle with toasted sesame seeds.

This is an adaptation of a classic Moroccan dish that was traditionally prepared with pigeon. You'll find that it freezes very well.

BBQ Duck Cakes
with Ginger, Lime and Pawpaw Salsa

Serves 6

2	Whole BBQ ducks
3 cloves	Garlic – minced
2 cm piece	Fresh ginger – grated
$\frac{1}{2}$ bunch	Fresh coriander – chopped roughly
$\frac{1}{2}$ tsp	Chinese five spice
1 tbls	Ketjap manis (Indonesian sweet soy)
1 tbls	Soy sauce
2	Eggs
3	Green shallots – chopped finely
1 tbls	Mango chutney
	Plain flour – for coating
	Vegetable oil – for shallow frying

Ginger, Lime and Pawpaw Salsa:

1	Ripe pawpaw (or 2 ripe mangoes) – peeled and seeded
	Juice of 2 limes
2	Green shallots – chopped finely
2 cm piece	Fresh ginger – minced
1	Chopped fresh red chilli – to taste
$\frac{1}{2}$ bunch	Fresh coriander
1	Lebanese cucumber – diced

Remove all the meat from the ducks, also keeping about one quarter of the skin. You won't need all the skin, but a little added to the duck cakes lends a wonderful sweetness and moistness.

Chop the meat and skin finely and place in a large bowl. Add the garlic, ginger, spring onions, coriander, eggs, soy sauce, Ketjap manis, chutney and five spice and mix through well. Shape the cakes and refrigerate till needed.

To prepare the salsa, cut the pawpaw into small cubes and toss through with the remaining salsa ingredients.

This is best made at least one hour before you need it so that all the flavours can mingle.

To cook the cakes, pass them through the flour to coat lightly.

In a large, heavy-based frying pan, heat a little vegetable oil and gently cook the duck cakes until they are crisp and golden on each side. Drain on absorbent paper. Serve hot with the salsa.

The aromatic flavours of the Chinese five spice work beautifully with the lime and pawpaw. You can purchase the duck at Asian food stores but, as to the inquiries of your admiring guests, of course you BBQ your own!

GUMBO YA YA
SERVES 6

6 cups	Hot cooked rice
3 tbls	Unsalted butter
3 tbls	Plain flour
1	Onion – chopped finely
3 cloves	Garlic – chopped finely
1	Small green capsicum – chopped
1	Small yellow capsicum – chopped
2 sticks	Celery – chopped
3	Large tomatoes – peeled and chopped
250g	Fresh okra – cut in halves lengthways
3 rashers	Bacon (rind off) – chopped
500g	Cooked prawns – peeled and deveined
500g	Cooked chicken – large dice
4 cups (1 Litre)	Chicken stock (hot)
2	Bay leaves
2 sprigs	Fresh thyme
$^1/_4$ tsp	Cayenne pepper
$^1/_4$ tsp	Ground black pepper
1 tbls	Worcestershire sauce
1 tbls	Filé powder (see Glossary, page 155)
	Parsley – for garnish
	Salt

Melt the butter in a large heavy-based saucepan, over a medium heat. Add the flour and cook it till the mixture (roux) starts to turn a deep golden colour (do not burn this mixture).

Add the onion, garlic, green and yellow capsicum, celery and bacon and cook for a few minutes, before gradually adding the hot chicken stock.

Once all the stock has been incorporated, add the tomatoes, okra, bay leaves and thyme.

Cook for a minute before adding the filé powder, worcestershire, cayenne and pepper.

Lower the heat and gently simmer for approximately 1 hour 10 minutes.

Before serving, add the chicken, adjust seasonings, adding salt to taste and, at the last minute, throw in the prawns just long enough for them to warm through. Serve the gumbo on a bed of white rice and garnish with freshly chopped parsley.

The Secret
The secret lies in the melting of the butter and the flour. You need to take it to a golden stage, just before it starts to turn a deep brown. This leaves a deliberate haunting flavour that evokes much of the gumbo's origins in the Deep South.

Gumbo filé is a special spice from the sassafras tree. Ya Ya means rice. The sauce can be made well in advance, just adding the cooked meat when required. A strong, slightly spicy sausage can be added as well, if you like.

ROBYN'S BRAISED LAMB SHANKS
WITH LEMON, OLIVES AND BASIL

SERVES 6

Allowing two lamb shanks per person makes for a very generous serving.

6–12	Lamb shanks
12	Small brown pickling onions – peeled and halved
2	Carrots – diced
1	Large red capsicum – cut into large dice
6	Tomatoes – peeled and cut into quarters
3 sticks	Celery – sliced finely
	Peeled rind of 2 lemons
24	Kalamata olives
3	Bay leaves
2 sprigs	Fresh thyme and/or rosemary
	A handful of fresh basil leaves
2 cups (500mL)	Red wine

Preheat the oven to 220°C. Place the shanks in a roasting tin and roast for 10–15 minutes to brown slightly. Remove from the tin and place in a large stockpot. Cover with cold water (or stock if you have it), and bring to the boil. Skim off excess fat and reduce to a slow simmer.

Add 1 chopped carrot, 1 stick celery, the bay leaves, thyme, the zest from the lemons and the red wine. Simmer for $1^1/_2$ hours and remember to keep skimming excess fat from the surface.

Remove the cooked carrot and celery and discard. Add the remaining carrot and celery, the onions, tomatoes and capsicum and simmer for a further 45 minutes.

Just before serving, add the olives and a generous amount of freshly chopped basil.

Serve with buttered couscous, polenta or boiled new potatoes.

This dish lends itself perfectly to being made in advance. In fact, it improves dramatically when eaten a day after cooking.

BBQ Lamb Kofta
with Couscous and Apricot Salad and Tahini and Yoghurt Dressing
Serves 6

1kg	Minced Lamb
1	Large onion – chopped finely
2	Eggs
2 cm piece	Fresh ginger – grated
2 cloves	Garlic – minced
1 tbls	Ketjap manis (Indonesian sweet soy)
$^1/_2$ tsp	Ras en hanout
	(see Glossary, page 155)
1 tbls	Ground cumin
2 tsp	Ground coriander
$^1/_2$ tsp	Ground allspice
$^1/_4$ tsp	Ground cinnamon
$^1/_4$ tsp	Chilli powder
$^1/_2$ bunch	Fresh coriander
	Salt and pepper

Mix all the ingredients together and set to one side for at least 2 – 3 hours in the refrigerator.

Mould the rested mixture into 5cm-long sausages and thread 2 to 3 on each of several skewers.

These are best BBQ'd, but they can be cooked under a grill or in a frying pan as well. They will take about 10–15 minutes, depending on your preference for pink or well done. Turn them a couple of times during the cooking to insure they are cooked and golden all over.

Serve warm with the cous cous salad and yoghurt sauce.

The kebabs can be made well in advance and kept in the refrigerator until needed.

Couscous and Apricot Salad

$^1/_2$ cup (100g)	Couscous
6	Ripe fresh apricots (or 15 drained, tinned apricots) – diced
1	Red capsicum – seeded and diced
1	Lebanese cucumber – diced
$^1/_2$ cup (80g)	Pine nuts – toasted
$^1/_2$ cup (80g)	Almonds – toasted and chopped
$^1/_2$ bunch	Coriander – chopped roughly
$^1/_2$ bunch	Flat-leaf parsley – chopped roughly
12 leaves	Mint – chopped roughly
1 tbls	Olive oil
$^1/_3$ cup	Balsamic vinegar
$^1/_3$ cup	Olive oil
$^1/_3$ cup	Hazelnut oil

To prepare the salad, place the couscous in a bowl, add 1 tablespoon of olive oil and rub through. Cover in boiling water for approximately 12 minutes, keep under a lid except when running a fork through occasionally to keep the grains separated.

Combine the cucumber, apricots, red capsicum, coriander, parsley, and mint. Gently mix these together with the toasted nuts. Stir together the $^1/_3$ cup olive oil and the vinegar and stir into the vegetables with the couscous. Mix through gently and serve at room temperature.

This salad can be made in advance, adding the vinaigrette just prior to serving.

Tahini and Yoghurt Dressing

1 cup (250mL)	Greek-style plain yoghurt
2 tbls	Tahini
1 tbls	Honey

To prepare the dressing, mix together the yoghurt, tahini and honey and set to one side until needed and spoon over the lamb.

An ideal dish for entertaining, you can buy the kebabs ready-made if you are in a hurry.

Desserts

* Semolina and Yogurt Cake
* Caramelised Yogurt Cream
* Andrew's Mango Jelly with Passionfruit and Strawberry Salad
* Pear and Ginger Cheesecake
* Blood Plum and Almond Upside Down Cake
* Pat's Coconut and Lemon Syrup Cake
* Lemon Curd Tart
* Trifle of Fresh Peaches and Nectarines with Ricotta Cream
* Florentine Squares
* Joan Campbell's Melting Moments
* Almond Biscotti with Vin Santo and Mascarpone
* Passionfruit Tart
* Creme Caramel
* Warm Date and Walnut Cake with Caramel Sauce

SEMOLINA AND YOGHURT
CAKE WITH CARAMELISED YOGHURT CREAM

MAKES A 24 CM ROUND CAKE

2 cups (250g)	Fine semolina
125g	Unsalted butter – softened
$^3/_4$ cup (185g)	Caster sugar
$^3/_4$ cup (185mL)	Yoghurt (Jalna apricot yoghurt is ideal)
2	Eggs
1 tsp	Baking powder
$^1/_2$ tsp	Bicarbonate of soda (baking soda)
1 tsp	Orange flower water (optional)
	Grated zest of 1 Lemon

SYRUP:

2 cups (500g)	Sugar
1 $^1/_2$ cups (375mL)	Water
1 tbls	Lemon juice
	Caramelised Yoghurt Cream

Preheat the oven to 180°C. Prepare a 24cm springform tin.

Beat the butter, caster sugar, orange flower water and lemon zest till light and fluffy. Add the eggs, one at a time, and beat well.

Sift together the semolina, baking powder and bicarbonate of soda thoroughly. Fold into the butter mixture alternately with the yoghurt.

Pour the mixture into the prepared tin and bake for 30–35 minutes, or until the cake is cooked when tested, with a skewer.

Meanwhile to prepare the syrup, dissolve the sugar in the water over medium heat. Add the lemon juice and bring to the boil. Boil rapidly for 10 minutes, then cool by placing the pan in cold water.

When the cake is cooked, spoon the cooled syrup over the hot cake.

Serve with caramelised yoghurt cream (recipe follows).

Not on the same time scale as wine admittedly, but this cake does actually improve with age, the syrup keeping it lovely and moist. It doubles as a great dessert served with poached or fresh fruit.

CARAMELISED YOGHURT
CREAM

$^1/_2$ cup (125mL)	Whipping cream
$^1/_2$ cup (125mL)	Thick, Greek-style yoghurt
	Brown sugar, to cover

To prepare the yoghurt cream, whip the cream till stiff and holding firm peaks then gently fold in the yoghurt.

Spoon the mixture into dishes (or dish) and cover with a thick layer of brown sugar.

Set in the fridge for at least 2 hours, the longer the better.

Simplicity strikes again. You won't believe how good this is.

ANDREW'S MANGO JELLY
WITH PASSIONFRUIT AND STRAWBERRY SALAD

SERVES 6–8

2$^1/_2$(800g)	Mango purée
	Juice of 2 oranges
3 leaves	Gelatine – softened
3	Passionfruit
1 punnet	Ripe, succulent strawberries or raspberries

Gently warm the orange juice and add the softened gelatine, mixing thoroughly so that no lumps remain.

Add this mixture to the mango purée and pour into a jelly mould.

Set in the fridge for at least 4 hours before turning out. The jelly will be quite soft so resist turning it out of the mould until just before needed.

To serve, wash the strawberries and pat dry. Remove the green hull and cut into fours.

Mix the berries with the passionfruit pulp and serve with the mango jelly.

This is a delicious summer pudding that is so easy to prepare and can be made up to one day in advance. Lovers of pawpaw may like to substitute it for the mango.

PEAR AND GINGER CHEESECAKE

MAKES ONE 24 CM ROUND CAKE

GINGER NUT BASE:

1 cup (200g)	Gingernut biscuits – crushed
$\frac{1}{3}$ cup (100g)	Almonds – crushed
125g	Butter – melted
1 tsp	Ground ginger

FILLING:

1 cup (250g)	Mascarpone
$\frac{1}{2}$ cup (125mL)	Whipped cream
	Dash of vanilla, or brandy
1 cup (250g)	Light Philadelphia cream cheese
3 tbls	Honey

FOR THE PEARS:

3	Pears – peeled and quartered
1 $\frac{1}{2}$ cups (375g)	Caster sugar
1 cup (250mL)	Water

Bring the sugar and water to the boil. Add the pears and poach till just softened. You don't want to over cook them.

Leave to cool in the syrup and, once cool, remove from syrup and roughly chop.

To prepare the Gingernut Base:
Combine all the ingredients and press mixture firmly into the base and sides of a lightly oiled 24cm springform tin. Chill this for at least 1 hour.

In a bowl, lightly beat the cream cheese.

Mix in the mascarpone, adding the honey and vanilla.

Gently fold through the whipped cream and the fully cooled, chopped pears.

Spread this cheese mixture onto the chilled biscuit base and return to the refrigerator for at least 3 hours before serving.

Delicious served with raspberries or blueberries.

Pear and ginger is a personal favourite, but you could just as easily use apples, quince, peaches or ripe mashed bananas. It's worth taking the time to crush your own almonds but purchased ground almonds can be sutstituted.

BLOOD PLUM AND ALMOND
UPSIDE DOWN CAKE
MAKES ON 23 CM ROUND CAKE

PLUMS:

8 – 12	Plums (according to size)
1 cup (220g)	Brown sugar
1 cup (250mL)	Water
4	Eggs
1	Vanilla bean – split and remove seeds for use
$1^1/_3$ cups (300g)	Brown sugar – firmly packed
150mL	Dry white wine
1 cup (250mL)	Olive oil
$2^1/_2$ cups (300g)	Plain flour
2 1/2 tsp	Baking powder
$^3/_4$ cup (120g)	Polenta
2 cups (450g)	Ground almonds

CARAMEL BASE:

$^2/_3$ cup (150g)	Raw sugar
$^1/_4$ cup (60mL)	Water

Bring the 1 cup brown sugar and 1 cup water to the boil and then gently poach the plums just long enough for them to soften slightly but retain their shape, probably 3–4 minutes.

Remove the plums from the syrup with a slotted spoon and allow to cool.

Cut in half and remove the stones.

Preheat the oven to 170°C.

Beat the eggs with the vanilla seeds and the $1^1/_3$ cups brown sugar until creamy and thick.

Beat in the oil and the white wine. Sift together the flour and baking powder and fold into the mixture with the polenta and ground almonds.

Mix through to form smooth batter.

For the caramel base:
Stir the water and raw sugar over a low heat until the sugar has dissolved.

Bring to the boil. Once the syrup starts to caramelise, pour onto the base of a deep, 23cm non-stick cake tin.

To assemble:
Place the plums, cheek-side-down, around the base of the tin, on top of the caramel syrup.

Pour in the cake batter. Place the tin on a flat baking tray and bake on the middle shelf of the oven till a skewer inserted in the centre comes away clean, 45 – 60 minutes.

Remove from the oven and leave to cool for at least 30 minutes before turning it out or it will crack.

If the toffee has set too hard, pass the tin over a naked gas flame for a minute or two to remelt the toffee. This is a fairly delicate operation to be done with great care.

Serve with double cream.

Variations:
Any stone fruit may be substituted, according to taste and availability.

The oil and wine give this cake its distinct lightness and quality.

desserts

137

PAT'S COCONUT AND LEMON
SYRUP CAKE
MAKES ONE 20CM ROUND CAKE

4	Eggs
125g	Butter
	Grated zest of 1 lime
	Grated zest of 1 lemon
1 cup (250g)	Caster sugar
2 cups (180g)	Desiccated coconut
1 cup (150g)	Self-raising flour
	LEMON SYRUP:
$^1/_2$ cup (125mL)	Water
$^3/_4$ cup (190g)	Sugar
	Juice 2 lemons
	Rind of 1 lemon – cut into strips

Preheat the oven to 180°C. Butter and flour a 20cm springform tin.

Cream the butter, caster sugar, lime and lemon zest together until light and fluffy.

Gradually add the eggs one at a time and beat till they are fully incorporated.

Fold in the coconut and the sifted flour.

Spoon the mixture into the prepared tin and bake for 45 minutes or until a skewer inserted in the centre comes away clean.

Meanwhile prepare the syrup. Combine all the ingredients in a saucepan and stir with a wooden spoon until the sugar dissolves.

Bring to the boil and simmer for about 5 minutes.

When the cake is cooked, pour over the hot syrup and leave it to cool in the tin before turning it out. Serve with double cream.

My thanks to good friend Pat Birley for this recipe. Pat is undoubtedly one of the finest cake makers I know. Her cakes have that true homemade, old fashioned quality. (And that 'I don't know when to stop eating' quality).

LEMON CURD TART
SERVES 8–10

1 quantity	Pastry (see Basics, page 154)
	FILLING:
1 cup (250mL)	Lemon juice (or lime juice)
150g	Unsalted butter
1 cup (250g)	Caster sugar
4 Large	Eggs – lightly whisked
	Grated zest of 1 lemon
	Double cream – for serving

Preheat the oven to 160°C. Prepare the pastry, adding the sugar and vanilla as directed for sweet tarts and use it to line a 25cm fluted tart tin. Line the pastry with greaseproof paper and weigh down with dry beans before baking blind for 20–25 minutes.

Remove the beans and paper. You may find the pastry needs a further 5 minutes to completely cook through. Once cooked, allow to cool.

Combine the filling ingredients in a heavy-based saucepan and stir constantly over a gentle heat until the mixture has thickened enough to coat the back of the spoon. Do this slowly and gently, otherwise it will all curdle.

This curd can be poured into storage jars and refrigerated till needed or strained straight into the tart shell. Allow to cool completely before serving it with double cream and strawberries, or raspberries.

Overwhelmed by the sheer number of variations for this tart, I began to question including it in the book. Its omission, however, would leave such an incomplete impression of the cafe cake world that I had to decide otherwise. Enjoy.

TRIFLE OF FRESH PEACHES
AND NECTARINES WITH RICOTTA CREAM

SERVES 8

6	Egg yolks
$^1/_3$ cup (100g)	Caster sugar
$^2/_3$ cup (170mL)	Brandy or sherry
1 cup (250g)	Ricotta
3tbls	Maple syrup
18	Savoiardi biscuits (sponge fingers)
	POACHED FRUIT:
1 punnet	Fresh raspberries – for garnish
	Toasted, flaked almonds –
	for garnish
4	Ripe white peaches
4	Ripe nectarines
4 cups (1 Litre)	Water
1 cup (250g)	Sugar

For the fruit:
Bring the sugar and water to the boil. When the syrup is boiling, plunge the peaches and nectarines into the boiling syrup for 2 – 3 minutes to soften the fruit and help remove the skins. Once peeled, cover with the syrup and set to one side.

For the ricotta cream:
In a stainless steel bowl, whisk the egg yolks with the caster sugar and maple syrup, add the brandy or sherry and, over a saucepan of boiling water, whisk the egg mixture till it is thick and frothy. Remove from the heat and set to one side to cool down completely. When cool, gently fold in the fresh ricotta.

To assemble:
Remove the peaches and nectarines gently from the syrup and slice in half to remove the stones. Slice the peaches and nectarines into eighths.

In eight individual trifle glasses, gradually build up layers of the sliced fruit, the ricotta cheese and the biscuits that have been softened by passing them through some of the peach syrup. Finish with a layer of the ricotta cheese and serve garnished with fresh raspberries and flaked almonds.

desserts

139

This is a very easily prepared dessert, refreshingly delicious and rich at the same time. Peaches and nectarines happen to be my personal favourites, but any of the fresh summer fruits can be used, such as figs, plums, apricots, or even a mixture of berries.

FLORENTINE SQUARES

MAKES 12 SQUARES

1$\frac{1}{4}$ cup (185g)	Dark chocolate (good quality) – chopped
1 cup (125g)	Sultanas
2 cups (100g)	Cornflakes – crushed
$\frac{1}{2}$ cup (80g)	Roasted almonds – whole
$\frac{1}{3}$ cup (60g)	Dried apricots – chopped
$\frac{1}{4}$ cup (60g)	Glacé cherries – chopped
2 tbls (20g)	Glacé ginger – chopped
3 tbls (30g)	Glacé peel – chopped
1 cup (250mL)	Condensed milk – sweetened

Melt the chocolate in a heatproof bowl over a saucepan of hot water. Spread the chocolate evenly over the base of a greased (18 x 28cm) lamington tin lined with aluminium foil and refrigerate until the chocolate has set firmly.

Preheat the oven to 180°C. Mix all the other ingredients together, spread the mixture onto the chocolate base and bake for 15–20 minutes or until golden on top. Remember, this will continue to harden as it cools.

Remove from the oven and cool slightly before turning out and removing the foil.

Refrigerate until set. Cut into squares to serve.

A simplified and heartier version of the florentine biscuit. This can also be made in a cake tin and sliced through.

JOAN CAMPBELL'S
MELTING MOMENTS

MAKES 16 BISCUITS

BISCUITS:

250g	Unsalted butter – softened
4 tbls	Icing sugar
4 tbls	Cornflour
1$\frac{1}{2}$ cups (185g)	Plain flour

ICING:

1$\frac{1}{2}$ cups (185g)	Icing sugar
2 tbls	Butter – softened
1 tbls	Vanilla essence

Preheat the oven to 160°C.

For the biscuits:
Beat the butter and icing sugar together and then gradually beat in the cornflour and flour. Mix well.

Turn the dough onto a floured surface and roll out to a 1cm thickness.

Cut into rounds and place on a non-stick baking tray, making a small indent with the flat of a fork on each biscuit.

Bake for 10–15 minutes or until golden and firm.

Cool on a wire rack.

For the icing:
Beat the sugar and butter together until creamy and add the vanilla essence. Use the icing to sandwich two biscuits together and repeat until all biscuits are paired.

My thanks to Joan Campbell for this foolproof recipe. Joan gave it to me during a promotion of Australian food in Hong Kong with Anders Ousback. I was responsible for teaching some highly proficient pastry chefs the finer points of our beloved pavlova, anzac biscuits, lamingtons and melting moments! Quite a challenge, I can assure you.

ALMOND BISCOTTI
WITH VIN SANTO AND MASCARPONE

SERVES 4

2$^1/_4$ cups (280g)	Plain flour
$^3/_4$ cups (185g)	Caster sugar
1 $^1/_2$ tsp	Baking powder
2	Eggs
1	Egg yolk
$^3/_4$ cup (115g)	Whole unblanched almonds – chopped
	Milk – for glazing
	Pinch of salt
1 cup (250g)	Fresh Mascarpone – for serving
	Vin Santo – for serving

Preheat the oven to 220°C.

Mix together the dry ingredients, add the eggs and egg yolk and knead into a smooth dough. Divide into six parts, shaping each into an oval log shape. (Its best to keep the biscotti quite small for this particular dish, making dipping easy and keeping disintegration in the glass to a minimum).

Place the logs on two floured baking trays, brush well with the milk and bake until golden brown, about 20 minutes. Remove and cool slightly.

While the logs are still warm, cut into 1cm-thick slices and lay flat on the baking trays. Bake for another 5–6 minutes until crisp golden. Cool on a cake rack.

To serve, divide the mascarpone among four individual bowls, serve with four glasses of Vin Santo, and the almond biscotti.

Dip the biscotti into the mascarpone and then the Vin Santo.

Easy.

This is a traditional Italian way to finish a meal. Vin Santo is a Tuscan dessert wine made from grapes that have been left to dry through the winter. After processing, the wine is left to age in small oak casks for at least 5 years. You should be able to find it at most good bottle shops or Italian food and wine outlets.

You can make this dessert even simpler to put together by choosing to purchase ready made biscotti. However, as they are so easy to make, I strongly recommend the satisfaction that comes from homebaking.

PASSIONFRUIT TART

SERVES 8–10

1 quantity	Pastry (see Basics, page 154)
	FILLING:
18	Passionfruit
4	Eggs – lightly beaten
$^1/_3$ cup (100g)	Caster sugar
$^1/_2$ cup (125mL)	Cream
	Icing sugar – sifted for dusting
	Double cream – for serving

Preheat the oven to 160°C.

Prepare the pastry, adding the caster sugar and vanilla as directed for sweet tarts and use it to line a 20cm fluted tart tin.

Line the pastry with greaseproof paper and weigh down with dry beans before baking blind for 10–15 minutes. Remove the beans and paper.

To make the filling:
Pass the pulp of the passionfruit through a sieve to remove the seeds and measure about $^1/_3$ cup (80mL) of juice. Reserve any extra pulp for the garnish.

Combine the passionfruit juice and sugar together in a bowl, add the eggs and finally the cream. Whisk together well.

Strain the mixture into the tart case and continue to bake on the middle oven shelf for 40–45 minutes, or till set. Remove from the oven.

When cool, sprinkle with icing sugar and serve with any extra passionfruit pulp and double cream.

This is a wonderfully easy tart to make, perfect for mid-summer when passionfruit are at their absolute sweetest and juiciest.

CRÈME CARAMEL

SERVES 6

	FOR THE CARAMEL:
$^3/_4$ cup (185g)	Caster sugar
$^3/_4$ cup (185mL)	Water
	FOR THE CUSTARD:
2 cups (500mL)	Milk
3	Eggs
3	Egg yolks
$^1/_2$ cup (125g)	Caster sugar
1	Vanilla bean – split

To make the caramel:
Dissolve the sugar and water in a heavy-based stainless steel saucepan. Bring to the boil and cook until the sugar begins to turn to a dark, caramel colour. Don't overcook at this stage as the caramel will continue to cook and darken when it is removed from the heat. Pour the caramel into the base of six dariole moulds.

Preheat the oven to 120°C.

To make the custard:
Bring the milk to scalding point with the vanilla bean, then leave to cool for a couple of minutes before removing the bean.

Beat the eggs and yolks together with the $^1/_2$ cup sugar. Strain the milk into the mixture and whisk gently, not to cause too much aeration or bubbles.

Divide this mixture evenly among the six dariole moulds.

Place the moulds into a baking tin and fill with warm water so that each dariole mould is two thirds immersed. Cover with aluminium foil and bake for 30–35 minutes or until the custard is just set.

Remove from the pan and allow to cool completely before turning out. It is preferable to chill them for at least one hour after they have cooled.

Serve with freshly sliced oranges and strawberries.

This well-loved dessert is one of the very first things I learned to cook and I still delight in its simplicity and unique charm. My husband has been known to find extraordinary satisfaction eating this for breakfast!

WARM DATE AND WALNUT
CAKE WITH CARAMEL SAUCE
SERVES 8–10

2 cups (250g)	Plain flour
2 tsp	Baking powder
225g	Unsalted butter
1 cup (250g)	Brown sugar
2	Eggs well beaten
1	Granny Smith – peeled and grated
1^1/$_2$ cups (150g)	Walnuts – chopped
1 cup (185g)	Dates – chopped
1 tsp	Bicarbonate of soda (baking soda)
1 cup (250mL)	Warm water
	CARAMEL SAUCE:
1^1/$_2$ cups (350g)	Brown sugar
200g	Unsalted butter
^{3}/$_4$ cup (200mL)	Cream
^{1}/$_2$ tsp	Vanilla or brandy

Dissolve the bicarbonate of soda in the warm water and pour over the chopped dates. Set to one side for at least one hour, longer if possible (up to six hours).

Preheat the oven to 180°C. Butter and flour a rectangular cake tin (18 x 28cm). Sift the flour and the baking powder together.

Cream the butter and sugar together till light and fluffy. Beat in the eggs one at a time, beating well after each addition.

Mix the dates, grated apple and walnuts together and mix this into the butter mixture by hand, alternatively with the flour.

Pour mixture into the prepared tin. Bake in the centre of the oven for 45–60 minutes or until a skewer inserted in the centre comes away clean.

To make the Caramel Sauce:
Bring all the ingredients to the boil, then reduce the heat and simmer gently for 3–4 minutes.

Serve the cake warm with the caramel sauce and double cream.

The sauce can be made in advance and gently reheated in a saucepan or microwave. What's more, this is where the microwave comes into its own for reheating cakes. One minute, ting, fresh as a daisy!

This would have to be one of the most universally loved sweets, vying only with the Lemon Curd Tart (recipe page 138) for supreme position.

basics

143

basics

* Gaucamole
* Parmasan and Gruyére Crisps
* Mustard Fruits
* Polenta
* Couscous
* Béchamel
* Toasted Coconut
* Oven Roasted Tomatoes
* Mashed Potatoes
* Zucchini Pickle
* Spicy Tomato Chutney
* Korean Dressing
* Thai Dressing
* Olive and Rosmary Bread
* Pastry for Savoury and Sweet Tarts
* Garlic Croutes
* Tomato Sauce
* Caramelised Onions
* Roasted Capsicum
* Balsamic Dressing
* Plain Vinaigrette
* Horseradish Dressing
* Pesto

* Caesar Dressing
* Gremolata
* Salsa Verde
* Mayonnaise
* Tapenade
* Aioli
* Walnut Biscotti
* Créme Anglaise
* Champagne Sabayon

GUACAMOLE

2 Ripe avocados

3 Radishes – diced very finely

2 Shallots – chopped finely

1 clove Garlic – minced

1 Green chilli – seeded and chopped
  finely

1 Tomato (ripe) – chopped finely

Coriander (a handful) – chopped

Juice 1 lime

Salt and pepper

In a bowl, mash the ripe avocados with a fork
and mix in the other ingredients. It is good to
make this a little ahead of time, so that the
flavours have time to mingle.

PARMESAN AND GRUYÉRE CRISPS
MAKES 12

$1^3/_4$ cups (180g) Parmesan – freshly
  grated

$1^3/_4$ cups 180g Gruyère cheese – freshly
  grated

Preheat the oven to 220ºC.

Mark out twelve 14cm circles on baking
paper and use to line baking trays. The size
of your oven, and the availability of baking
trays, will determine how many batches you
will need to do this in.

Mix the cheeses and sprinkle generously
over the marked circles.

Bake for 10 minutes, or till each of the
cheese rounds has melted and can be lifted
off with a flexible spatula.

Remove from the oven and allow to cool for a
minute before removing from the baking
trays and cooling further on a wire rack.

Variations:
* Sprinkle with cayenne pepper, fennel
  seeds, poppy seeds or fresh sage leaves.

* Mould them over a rolling pin or in a
  dariole mould to create different shapes.

This is best done 30 seconds after they have
been removed from the oven.

*A simple and extremely memorable
accompaniment for salads, soups or
risottos.*

MUSTARD FRUITS

2 Cups (500g) White sugar

1 Cup (250mL) Water

1kg Mixed glacé fruits, such as apricots,
  peaches, cherries, ginger, figs

2 tsp Mustard seeds

3 Quills cinnamon

6 Cloves

2 Bay leaves

$^3/_4$ cup 150mL White wine vinegar

$^1/_2$ cup 60g Dry mustard powder

In a heavy-based saucepan, combine
$1^2/_3$ cups of the sugar with the water and
stir over a medium heat till the sugar is
completely dissolved.

Add the spices and the fruit, left in whole
pieces, and cook over a gentle heat for
8–10 minutes.

Remove the fruit with a slotted spoon and
keep to one side.

Add the remaining sugar and vinegar to the
syrup, return to the heat and cook till the
syrup is lovely and thick.

Remove from the heat and stir in the
mustard powder.

Let the syrup cool for about an hour before
pouring over the glacé fruit and storing in
sterilised jars.

It is best to make this at least a couple of
days before needed and, like most pickles
and chutneys, the flavours are found to
greatly improve with a little shelf life.

*Mustard fruits, a specialty of Cremona in
Italy, are known for their wonderful
accompaniment to cold meats and terrines.
However, once made, be sure not to let
roasted pumpkin or seafood escape their
charms.*

POLENTA

SERVES 4–6

8 cups (2 litres) Water

$2^2/_3$–$2^2/_3$ cups (350 – 400g)
Polenta

2 cups (200g) Parmesan – freshly
grated

2 tbls Olive oil

2 tsp Salt

Bring the water to the boil with salt and olive oil. Reduce to simmer and slowly add polenta in a continuous stream, whisking all the time to avoid any lumps. Reduce to very low heat and stir with a wooden spoon. Be warned, polenta spits like an erupting volcano! Stir frequently and cook for about 20 minutes. Add the parmesan right at the end. Pour into a well oiled shallow tray and let cool.

Variations:
* For soft, wet polenta add 1 cup (250mL) milk to 1.75 Litres water, and when adding the cheese at the end, add 150g butter. Good with winter stews, etc.

* Sweat off leeks, garlic and red capsicum and add to the cooked polenta before the cheese.

* Use chicken stock instead of water.

* Add lots of fresh herbs, such as parsley, basil, rosemary or sage.

* Eat soft polenta with blue cheese, rosemary, mascarpone and parmesan.

COUSCOUS

SERVES 4–6

1 cup (185g) Couscous

1 tbls Olive oil

Place couscous in a bowl, add 1 tablespoon olive oil and rub through. Cover in boiling water for approx. 20 minutes with a sealed lid, running a fork through the couscous occasionally to keep grains separate.

Variations:
Depending on your intended use you can add all manner of ingredients, such as:

* Freshly chopped coriander, toasted almonds and sultanas.

* Ground cumin, coriander and ginger.

* Finely diced onion, carrot, celery and parsley.

BÉCHAMEL

MAKES 2 CUPS

60g Butter

$^1/_2$ cup (60g) Plain flour

500mL Milk or stock

Salt and pepper

Bring the liquid to the boil and remove from the heat.

Melt the butter in a heavy-based saucepan.

Add the flour and cook the roux for 2–3 minutes, stirring all the time.

Gradually incorporate all of the hot liquid.

Adjust the seasoning and cook over a low heat stirring for 15–20 minutes. Cheese can be added at this stage if desired.

An old fashioned flour thickened sauce that I still find very useful for pies, lasagnes, tortes, etc.

OVEN ROASTED TOMATOES

6–8 Ripe roma tomatoes

3 tbls Olive oil

1 tbls Balsamic vinegar

2 cloves Garlic – chopped finely

1 tbls Herbs such as rosemary, thyme
and sage – chopped fresh

Pinch of sugar

Salt and pepper

Preheat the oven to 160°C.

Cut the tomatoes in half, lengthways, and
place on a shallow baking tray.

Drizzle with the olive oil and balsamic
vinegar.

Scatter the garlic, herbs, sugar and salt and
pepper to taste over the tomatoes.

Roast for 1 hour, or till soft.

*Another kitchen staple that can be kept in
the fridge to be used on any occasion.*

MASHED POTATOES
SERVES 4–6

500g Potatoes
(Sebago are my particular favourite)

1 stick Celery – cut in to four

4 cloves Garlic – peeled

150g Butter

3 tbls Olive oil

$^3/_4$ cup (200mL) Cream or milk

Salt and pepper

Cover the potatoes, celery, and garlic in a
saucepan with cold salted water.

Bring to the boil and simmer gently until
potatoes are soft.

Drain and discard the celery.

Mash the potatoes with the butter and olive
oil, adding the cream as necessary.

Finish with salt and pepper.

This can be made in advance and warmed
through with a little extra milk or cream.

*Cooking good mashed potatoes really does
rely on the feeling and taste relationship.
Since all potatoes vary in their starchiness,
you will find that you need to vary these
quantities from time to time—more cream
here, a little bit more olive oil and butter
there. The celery and garlic both lend
enormous flavour whilst the potatoes are
cooking but the celery should be discarded
before mashing. It is also very important
not to overwork the potatoes in the mashing
process. Use a good old fashioned potato
masher, fork or a mouli. Never be tempted
to use a food processor or blender the
result will be like glue.*

ROASTED CAPSICUMS

2 Capsicums (red)

1 tbls Olive oil

3 cloves Garlic

2 sprigs Thyme (optional)

Preheat the oven to 200°C.

Place capsicums in baking tray with 3 whole
cloves of garlic (unpeeled). Drizzle with oil
and put in oven for 30–40 minutes, turning
frequently to prevent burning.

When fully roasted remove from oven and
place in bowl, covering with plastic wrap—
this step helps steam off the skin.

When cool enough to handle, remove the
seeds, keeping the flesh in as large pieces
as possible.

*The oil and juices collected from the
cooking process go really well in salad
dressings, brushed onto wood-fired bread
prior to toasting, or added to a pasta
sauce.*

CARAMELISED ONIONS

1kg Small brown pickling onions

$^1/_2$ cup (125g) Sugar

1 cup (250mL) Vinegar
   (preferably white wine)

100mL Olive oil

1 tbls Butter

Blanch and peel the onions.

In a heavy-based saucepan, heat the vinegar, olive oil and sugar.

When the sugar turns a light golden colour, add the onions, slowly, to prevent splashing the caramel.

Toss thoroughly, ensuring that each onion is will coated. Reduce heat and slowly caramelise, stirring occasionally to keep the onions well coated. Depending on the size of the onions, this should take between 20–40 minutes.

Alternatively, onions can be placed in the oven in a baking tin covered with aluminium foil and caramelised there. If heat is too vigorous, the caramel will reduce too quickly. If this happens, add some water and toss vigorously once again.

Store in fridge.

TOMATO SAUCE

500g Fresh ripe tomatoes – blanched,
   peeled and seeded

1 Onion – sliced finely

1 Carrot – diced

1 stick Celery – chopped

3 cloves Garlic – minced

1 sprig Rosemary

1 sprig Thyme

100mL Olive oil

Pinch of brown sugar

Salt and pepper

In a large heavy-based saucepan, place all the ingredients and cook, covered, over a moderate heat for about 20–25 minutes, or till the onions and tomatoes have both softened. Remove the rosemary and thyme sprigs.

Pass the mixture through a food processor and process to suit your requirements; chunky or smooth.

It's worth multiplying the ingredients and making this up in bulk during the summer when tomatoes are at their most flavoursome. With a ready supply of frozen tomato sauce in your fridge, you'll never be stuck for a meal. Use it as a base for pasta sauce, casseroles and pizzas. This recipe, as it stands, will make enough for about 4 serves of pasta.

TOASTED COCONUT

Take one whole coconut and pierce 2 of the 3 round buttons at the top. Invert over a glass and collect the milk. This may be used to drink fresh or to add flavour to a Thai stock.

Do 'whatever it takes' to split the coconut open - smashing it with a hammer is probably one of the most efficient ways. Ideally, you will end up with 5 or 6 pieces.

The easiest way I have found to remove the coconut flesh from the shell is to wedge the tip of a sharp knife between the two layers in order to break the vacuum and, with a heavier kitchen knife, gently continue to lift the coconut from the shell.

Once you have your flesh, use a sharp vegetable peeler to shave the coconut into strips. These are then placed on a flat baking tray and cooked in a pre-heated oven at 180°C till they turn a lovely golden honey colour.

A whole coconut will produce a lot of shavings, so be sure to have other plans for using it, or freeze it for making coconut milk next time you need it.

If this all sounds like to much hassle, most good health food shops sell shaved coconut which you can then toast.

MICK'S SPICY TOMATO SALSA
SERVES 4–6

2 Ripe tomatoes (large)

1 Spanish (red) onion

1 Lebanese cucumber

$^1/_2$ Red capsicum (medium)

1 clove Garlic – minced

$^1/_2$ bunch Coriander – chopped

2 tbls Olive oil

2 tbls Cider vinegar

Chilli to taste – very finely chopped

Salt and pepper

Chop all the vegetables into small dice.

Add the garlic, olive oil, vinegar, salt, pepper, chilli, and the freshly chopped coriander. Make this at least 1 hour in advance.

GARLIC CROUTES

6 slices White bread –
    cut into 1cm cubes

2 cloves Garlic – roughly chopped

1 tbls Butter

1 tbls Olive oil

In a heavy-based frypan melt the butter with the olive oil and a add the garlic.

When this is sizzling gently, throw in the cubes of bread and toss continuously till they turn a light golden brown.

You may need a little extra oil or butter depending on the size of the bread and how dry it is.

ZUCCHINI PICKLE

1 kg Green zucchini (small)

2 Brown onions (large) –
    sliced very finely

3 tbls Salt

PICKLING SYRUP:

2 cups (440g) Raw sugar

1 cup (250mL) White wine vinegar

2 tsp Black mustard seeds

2 tsp Celery seeds

$1^1/_2$ tsp Turmeric

$^1/_2$ tsp Chilli powder

$^1/_2$ tsp Ground cinnamon

With a vegetable peeler, shave long thin strips off the zucchini and place in a bowl.

Mix in the onions and salt and leave to stand for 2 hours then rinse the salt off thoroughly.

Bring all the syrup ingredients to the boil in a large, heavy-based saucepan and add the zucchini and onion.

Turn off the heat and leave to stand for 2 hours.

Bring the mixture back to the boil and transfer immediately into sterilised jars. Seal when cold.

Sealed, the pickle will last of 6 months in the fridge. Use in 3 or 4 weeks when opened.

Perfect with cold meats. This pickle also makes a colourful addition to an antipasto plate.

SPICY TOMATO CHUTNEY

2 kg Ripe tomatoes – peeled and
    chopped

2 Granny Smith apples – peeled and
    chopped

2 Brown onions (large) – chopped

1 cup (125g) Sultanas

$1^1/_2$ cups (345g) Brown sugar

5 cups (1.25L) Brown vinegar
    (or cider vinegar)

2 tsp Dry mustard powder

2 tsp Curry powder

2 tsp Ground ginger

$^1/_2$ tsp Ground cinnamon

$^1/_2$ tsp Ground cloves

$^1/_4$ tsp Cayenne pepper

In a large, stainless steel saucepan, combine all the ingredients and bring slowly to the boil, stirring continuously till all the sugar has dissolved.

Once boiling, reduce heat and simmer gently for $1^1/_2$ hours. The chutney should be nice and thick.

Pour into sterilised jars and seal when cold.

Sealed, the chutney could last as long as 12 months. Once opened, use within 8 weeks.

This chutney is a fabulous standby for the kitchen pantry. I particularly love it mixed with some vinaigrette and served with warm chicken and toasted almonds. Delicious also for sandwiches, casseroles and frittata.

BALSAMIC DRESSING

MAKES 1 CUP

$^2/_3$ cup (170mL) Olive oil

$^1/_3$ cup (80mL) Balsamic vinegar

Salt and pepper

Place the oil and vinegar in a bottle or jar and season with salt and pepper. Cover and shake vigorously.

PLAIN VINAIGRETTE

MAKES 1 CUP

$^2/_3$ cup (170mL) Olive oil

$^1/_3$ cup (80mL) White wine vinegar

1 tbls Dijon mustard

1 Egg yolk

Salt and pepper

Place the egg yolk in a bowl with the mustard and season with salt and pepper. Slowly whisk in the vinegar and mix thoroughly. Incorporate the olive oil gradually. Put in a bottle or jar. The Vinaigrette will keep in fridge for two weeks.

HORSERADISH VINAIGRETTE

MAKES 1 CUP (APPROXIMATELY)

1 clove Garlic – finely minced

1cm piece Glacé ginger – finely chopped

2 tsp Horseradish

2 tsp Dijon mustard

2 tbls Cider vinegar

4 tbls Extra virgin olive oil

1 tbls Caper juice – optional
   (from a jar of capers)

1 tbls Green olive juice – optional
   (from a jar of green olives)

1 tbls Chives – chopped

1 tbls Flat-leaf parsley – chopped

Mix all of the above by shaking in a sealed jar. This will keep in the fridge for 1 week.

MAYONNAISE

MAKES 2 CUPS (APPROX.)

3 Egg yolks

2 tsp White wine vinegar

1 tbls Dijon mustard

200mL Olive oil

200mL Vegetable oil

Salt and pepper

Whisk together the egg yolks, mustard, vinegar and a pinch of salt.

Slowly dribble in the olive and vegetable oil, whisking all the time.

When the oils are fully incorporated, whisk in 2 tablespoons of warm water to stabilise the mayonnaise.

Add pepper to taste.

There is no substitute for homemade mayo. Make up a jar and keep it in the fridge so its always on hand.

CAESAR DRESSING

MAKES 1 CUP

2 Egg yolks

$^3/_4$ – 1 cup (185–250mL) Olive oil

2 cloves Garlic – peeled

2 Anchovy fillets

$2^1/_2$ tsp Dijon mustard

$2^1/_2$ tbls (50mL) White wine vinegar

Salt and pepper

Place the egg yolks in a food processor with the mustard, salt and pepper and process briefly to blend.

Add the vinegar and garlic and continue to process, while slowly adding the olive oil.

Once all the oil has been added, blend in the anchovies and their oil.

No cafe menu seems complete these days without the ubiquitous caesar salad. Here is my simplified version of this classic dressing. For those not partial to the salty seduction of the anchovy, it is easily omitted but it is not quite the same.

PESTO

SERVES 4–6

2 bunches (240g) Basil leaves –
   picked from stalks

2 cloves Garlic

2 tbls Pine nuts

$^1/_2$ cup (125mL) Olive oil

1 cup (100g) Parmesan –
   freshly grated

Salt and pepper

Place the basil leaves, garlic, pine nuts and salt and pepper to taste in a food processor. Process, scraping down the sides, to ensure thorough blending of ingredients. Add the olive oil and finally the cheese.

A personal survey reveals that for most people, their first taste experience of pesto was so wonderful that they can recall with ease when and where they were for that first bite.
This delicious kitchen staple freezes well. Add a frozen ice block of pesto to lift a vegetable soup, or melt some into a creamy sauce for a pasta. A tablespoon of fresh pesto in vinaigrette or mayonnaise will transform a salad.

AIOLI

MAKES 1 CUP (APPROXIMATELY)

5 cloves Garlic

2 Egg yolks

1 tbls Dijon mustard

2 tbls White wine vinegar

1 cup (250mL) Olive oil

Salt

Roast the garlic cloves in their skins until soft. Remove the skins and mash. Place the garlic, egg yolks, vinegar, mustard and salt in a food processor. Blend the ingredients and, with the machine running, slowly incorporate the olive oil in a slow stream.

A quick alternative is to simply add some minced garlic to your homemade mayonnaise. It's a different result but delicious nonetheless.

GREMOLATA

Zest of 2 or 3 lemons
   (depending on size) – finely grated

1 clove Garlic – chopped finely with salt

$^1/_2$ bunch Flat-leaf parsley – chopped

Mix the ingredients and sprinkle over cooked lamb.

A bright lift to BBQ fish and lamb or grilled vegetables.

TAPENADE

MAKES 2 CUPS (APPROXIMATELY)

2 cups (300g) Kalamata olives – pitted

$^1/_2$ Red capsicum

$^1/_2$ Tomato – seeded

2 cloves Garlic

50g Capers

2 Green shallots

1/4 bunch Flat-leaf parsley – chopped

$2^1/_2$ tbls Extra virgin olive oil

2 Anchovy fillets (optional)

Chop the olives, capsicum, tomato, garlic, capers and shallots very finely. Add the chopped parsley and slowly incorporate the olive oil, and anchovies, if using. Use a splash of balsamic vinegar, if preferred.

The Secret

Its really important to use good quality, delicious olives here and, to my taste, you can't beat kalamata.

This variation on tapenade is particularly good with bruschetta or wood-fired crostini. Mixed with a little mayonnaise, it becomes a wonderful dressing for a tomato salad or grilled chicken.

SALSA VERDE

MAKES 1 CUP (APPROXIMATELY)

1 Egg – hard-boiled

1 tbls Dijon mustard

3 cloves Garlic

100g Capers

100g Anchovy fillets

1 bunch (150g) Flat-leaf parsley – chopped

1 bunch (120g) Basil – chopped

$2^1/_2$ tbls (50mL) White wine vinegar

$^1/_2$ cup (100mL) Extra virgin olive oil

Lemon juice – to taste

Salt and pepper

Place the boiled egg, mustard and vinegar in a food processor.

Add the garlic, capers, anchovies and herbs and pulse till combined.

Then, with the machine running, slowly incorporate the olive oil.

Season with salt, pepper and lemon.

Its hard to beat the simplicity of this sauce with BBQ fish or seafood. I love it spread generously on Italian wood-fired bread.

THAI DRESSING

1 tbls Crushed palm sugar (jaggery) (see Glossary, page 154)

Juice of 3–4 limes

4 tbls Rice vinegar or coconut vinegar

3 cloves Garlic – chopped finely

5 cm piece Lemon grass – chopped finely

2 Kaffir lime leaves – julienned

3 cm piece Ginger – chopped finely or grated

1 tbls Fish sauce

2 Coriander roots – chopped

2 – 6 Green chillies (according to taste) – chopped

Break the palm sugar down with a mortar and pestle by adding the lime juice and the vinegar.

Transfer to bigger bowl and add the other ingredients.

Set aside for 30 minutes before using.

Thai Dressing can be kept refrigerated in a sealed jar for up to 3 weeks. Delicious with BBQ chicken, octopus or prawns.

KOREAN DRESSING

$^1/_2$ tsp Finely grated fresh ginger

1 clove Garlic – chopped finely

2 tsp Sesame oil

2 tbls Ketjap manis
(Indonesian sweet soy)

4 tbls Light soy

2 tbls Sweet chilli sauce

4 tbls Vegetable oil

2 tbls Rice vinegar

Lots of black pepper – to taste

Place all the ingredients in a bowl and mix well.

This dressing can be kept refrigerated in a sealed jar for up to two months.

CRÈME ANGLAISE
MAKES 3 CUPS (APPROXIMATELY)

$2^1/_2$ cups Milk

6 Egg yolks

$^1/_2$ cup (110g) Sugar

$^1/_2$ tsp Vanilla essence

Bring the milk to the boil with the vanilla.

Beat the egg yolks with the sugar in a bowl until light and creamy.

Pour the milk onto the egg mixture and whisk well.

Return the mixture to the saucepan and stir continuously with a wooden spoon over a low heat. Cook gently until the egg mixture coats the back of the wooden spoon.

Strain the custard and serve either warm or cold, depending on taste and requirement.

Crème Anglaise is really just a refined custard that lends itself beautifully to so many desserts and cakes. For different flavours, ginger for example, just add a few slices of ginger when boiling the milk. Orange or lemon peel would be other alternatives. Ground coffee, almonds or apple purée are best added once the crème anglaise has cooled down. If you ever have any leftover, it can be used as the base for ice cream.

CHAMPAGNE SABAYON
MAKES $1^1/_2$ CUPS (APPROXIMATELY)

6 large Egg yolks

$^1/_4$ cup (60g) Caster sugar

1 cup (250mL) Champagne

Whisk the egg yolks and sugar together in a heatproof bowl till they are pale. Add the champagne and then set the bowl over a saucepan of just boiling water, and whisk continuously until the sabayon is thick and foamy. Remove from heat and cool thoroughly.

The Secret
'Champagne' sabayon can be made perfectly well with white wine and either lemonade or some fizzy mineral water.

PASTRY FOR SAVOURY AND SWEET TARTS

MAKES ONE 20 CM TART

If making pastry for sweet tarts, such as the Lemon Curd or Passionfruit Tarts (recipes, pages 138 and 142), add 60g of caster sugar and a teaspoon of vanilla essence to the flour mixture prior to adding the butter.

200g Unsalted butter (cold)

2 cups (250g) Plain flour

3 tbls Iced water

1 Egg yolk

Pinch of salt

Sift the flour and salt together into a large stainless steel bowl. Chop the butter into small cubes and gently rub flour and butter together till you have what looks like rough breadcrumbs.

Beat the yolk and the water together.

Create a well in the centre of the flour and butter mixture.

Pour in the water. Mix and quickly work to bring all the ingredients together to form a smooth dough.

Wrap this dough in plastic wrap and refrigerate for at least 30 minutes before using. (Do not omit this stage).

This pastry both freezes very well and can easily be made in a food processor, taking great care not to overwork any of the steps.

The essential points for good pastry making are that the butter is cold (straight from the fridge) and that your hands are not too warm, or else a tough pastry will result instead of a light and crispy one. And it is very important that the combining of the flour and butter mixture with the water and egg is not overdone.

You'll find this to be a very versatile pastry, lending itself well to all sorts of pies and tarts.

OLIVE AND ROSEMARY BREAD

MAKES 4–6 TART SHELLS

Many thanks to Jill Dupleix, from whose wonderful book New Food this recipe is borrowed.

$1^1/_2$ cups (185g) Plain flour

$^1/_2$ tsp Salt

1/2 tsp Baking powder

$^1/_2$ Onion – sliced

1/2 cup (75g) Kalamata olives – seeded

1 tbls Fresh rosemary leaves

$^1/_2$ tbls Parmesan – grated

1 tbls Butter

$^1/_4$ cup (60mL) Milk

Sift the flour, salt and baking powder into a large bowl.

Add the onion slices, olives, rosemary and cheese.

Mix through with your hands.

Melt the butter until frothy, add to the flour mixture with the milk, mixing to a smooth dough.

Knead dough a few times and set aside to rest in the fridge.

Now, those of you following this recipe to prepare Roasted Tomato and Olive Tart can return to page 87 at this point.

If, however, you're baking this bread as an accompaniment for a soup or, perhaps, antipasto, proceed as follows.

Divide the dough into 4 equal balls and roll each on a lightly floured bench.

Brush each one with melted butter.

Using a non-stick baking sheet, bake for 10 minutes at 200°C, then turn them over for a further 5 minutes.

WALNUT BISCOTTI

250g Butter (at room temperature)

1 cup (250g) Sugar

6 Eggs

$5^1/_4$ cups (650g) Plain flour

2 tbls Cumin seeds – toasted

3 tbls Caraway seeds (or fennel seeds)

2 cups (250g) Walnuts – chopped

2 tsp Salt

1 tbls Baking powder

Preheat the oven to 180°C.

In a bowl, beat the sugar and butter until fluffy.

Add the eggs, one at a time and beat well.

Sift together the flour, baking powder and salt, add to the egg mixture with the caraway seeds, cumin seeds and walnuts and mix till combined.

Form the mixture into 2 or 3 oval logs, place on non-stick biscuit trays and bake until golden brown and firm to touch, 30–35 minutes.

Remove from the oven and allow to cool for about 10 minutes.

Reduce the oven temperature to 120°C.

Cut the logs into slices ($1^1/_2$–2cm), lay on baking trays and bake until dry, crisp and golden, about 8–10 minutes. Cool completely.

These will store well for a couple of days in a sealed jar. However, if they do go a bit 'soggy' simply return them to a hot oven for a few minutes and let them dry out again. This said, they are so delicious that I don't anticipate them hanging around that long.

glossary

ACIDULATED WATER
Water to which lemon juice or vinegar has been added. Used to prevent certain fruits and vegetables, such as apples, pears, artichokes, from browning.

BLANCHING
A common cooking practice whereby food is plunged into boiling water for a few moments and then immediately refreshed under cold water. This helps vegetables retain their colour and texture.

DEEP-FRIED BEAN CURD CAKES
(Dow Foo Pok)—Bean curd made from soy beans, high in protein and used extensively in Japanese and Asian cuisine. Deep-fried bean curd cakes can be bought 'ready-fried' and are used to garnish laksas, soups, gado gado, curries, etc.

FILÉ
Spice from the sassafras tree used in gumbo. Available from specialty delicatessens.

GHEE
Clarified butter used mainly in India. Butter in which the salt and milk products have been removed enabling it to be heated to a much higher degree before burning.

GOMASIO
Ground sesame seeds mixed with salt and sometimes monosodium glutamate. Commonly used as a flavour and garnish with Japanese food. Available from Asian food stores.

GREEN SHALLOTS
Also known as green onions and are frequently sold as plain shallots. Picked when immature, the white bulb at the base of the long green stems is quite small.

HALOUMI
A hard goat's or sheep cheese that lends itself well to being grilled or baked. Available from good delicatessens and cheese shops.

KAFFIR LIME LEAVES
(Asian Lime)—Leaves are used to flavour and garnish soups, salads and curries. Available fresh, dried, or frozen (frozen being much the inferior).

KETJAP MANIS
(or Kecap Manis)—Sweet Indonesian soy sauce available at all Asian food stores and major supermarkets. It's worth investing in this delicious sauce as it brings such a distinctive touch to so many recipes, quite different from Chinese soy. If you can't find it, mix 100mL of light soy with a tablespoon of palm sugar.

KRUPUK
Deep fried prawn crackers. Small pink disks that, when plunged into hot oil, swell and puff up like pappadums. Can be bought ready cooked.

LEBANESE CUCUMBERS
Small green cucumbers. The seeds and skin are edible.

PALM SUGAR
Also known as Jaggery. The reduced sap of coconut and palmyran trees. Available from Asian supermarkets, it comes in a solid form from which required amounts can be sliced. It stores well and has a wonderfully distinct sweetness

PANCETTA
Traditionally-cured Italian bacon, sold in varying grades and quality. Eaten raw like prosciutto or cooked like streaky bacon.

PICKLING ONIONS
Small, round, brown skinned onions available in autumn and winter. Like green shallots, these are picked before they are fully grown

PORCINI MUSHROOMS
Strong, earthy-flavoured mushroom sold dried in Australia. Having been soaked before use, the soaking water may be used for flavouring.

RAS EN HANOUT

A mixture of spices and herbs from Northern Africa that can vary considerably according to the region and the particular spice merchant that has prepared it. It can be quite difficult to find in Australia but some specialty spice shops do stock it. There's nothing like the real thing but when the real thing can't be found, substitute it with a mild curry powder.

SEMOLINA

Very fine ground wheat used mostly in cakes and puddings. Italians use it for making gnocchi.

SHRIMP PASTE

Known as Blacan, Belacan, Kapi or Mam Tom depending on the country of origin. A southeast Asian ingredient that can be bought dried or in paste form—dried is stronger. It has an overwhelming smell that may have you wondering why on earth you would use it but, happily, this dissipates during cooking.

STAR ANISE

Small, star-shaped spice carrying a strong aniseed flavour.

TAHINI

Paste made from roasted sesame seeds, used extensively in middle-eastern cookery. Available from health food shops and most good supermarkets.

TAMARIND

Tamarind has a unique flavour that is well worth acquainting yourself with — sour, yet full of depth. Tamarind water is prepared by breaking off a small block of tamarind, washing it and covering it with warm water for 10 minutes before squeezing the flesh through a strainer back into the water. This will keep refrigerated for one week.

TORTILLAS

Mexican bread made from corn or wheat, Flat and round, it is traditionally used for wrapping foods. Available from good supermarkets.

WASABI

Dried, green Japanese horseradish, very strong in flavour. Eaten with sushi and sashimi or it can be mixed into mayonnaises, dressings, dips.

index